Teaching:
From Command
to Discovery

Muska Mosston

Teaching Behavior Institute*

Wadsworth Publishing Company, Inc.
Belmont, California

*275 Floral Drive
Somerville, N.J. 08876

ISBN–0–534–00165–3
L. C. Cat. Card No.: 70–186944
Printed in the United States of America

4 5 6 7 8 9 10–76 75

This book has been printed on recycled paper.

To my dear colleague and friend
Rudy Mueller
whose sensitivity and patience helped
sustain me in moments of agony
and joy along the road

Acknowledgment

I would like to thank Dr. Frank W. Kovacs of the N.E.A., Dr. Norma Furst of Temple University, Dr. M. Lawrence Furst of Villanova University and Dr. Paul Torrance of the University of Georgia for their insightful and encouraging reviews of the manuscript.

I would also like to extend my gratitude to my editor, Kevin Gleason, for his corrections and patience.

Foreword

"From Command to Discovery"—in every age, there have been advocates of some new variation in teaching styles ranging along the continuum from command to discovery. As I interpret the accumulated research and experience of the ages, we can expect no supreme style that will serve every teacher and every learner. A style generally successful may be altogether unsuccessful when used by another teacher. A style generally successful with most children may be quite damaging for some children.

A teacher's way of teaching *must* be his or her own personal creation. It should be suited to his or her personality, special talents, and skills. Regardless of the dominant theme of a teacher's way of teaching, one's way of teaching should include a wide repertoire of styles to give every child a chance to learn and to develop a wide range of his own talents. Otherwise, some children will fail to learn altogether and even the most successful will develop only a few of his intellectual abilities and talents.

Saying that a teacher's way of teaching must be his or her personal creation should not convey the idea that the research, theory, and experience of the ages is worthless. Even the most imaginative and inventive teacher will find guidance in this accumulation of knowledge. Such a teacher, however, will bring to bear upon this knowledge his insights and intuitions about himself—his talents, skills, motivations, interests—his individuality. He will also use his understandings about the nature of man, the functioning of the human mind, the nature of human development, and the like.

A careful examination of the alternatives in teaching styles that Muska Mosston offers in this book could be useful to any teacher at any stage of development. Such an examination should help inoculate a teacher against blind acceptance of today's educational prophets who boldly urge that teachers lay aside considerations about human dignity and freedom. Muska Mosston, in presenting styles ranging from command to discovery, shows respect for the dignity and freedom of both teachers and learners and provides a useful vehicle for examining the issues that must be decided in inventing one's way of teaching.

E. Paul Torrance

To the Reader

This book began long ago — not the actual ideas, nor the educational models and jargon, but the profound feelings that many of my teachers mistreated me, the intense sensation that teaching could develop a relationship which evokes invitation and inclusion rather than rejection and exclusion.

As a kid I could never understand why teachers were unable to let us daydream, play with our thoughts, and express what we felt. When I grew older I understood this even less. As a student of education and psychology I observed the gaping discrepancy between what some of my professors preached and what they actually did in the classroom. In teaching children and college students and in conducting programs for people who were blind, brain-damaged, or disturbed I could not help but realize the struggle I had in confronting the dogma of institutions, the sterility of sameness in some theories and the crippling power of over-rated traditions.

I have always been struck by the single-dimension theories and ideas that flood the educational scene. I have always stood in awe of the contributions of many thinkers but I have always been puzzled by the insistence with which each has promoted a theory, a model, a conception *versus* all the others. After all, human beings *are* variable creatures — their thoughts, feelings, social patterns never have adhered (and I hope never will) to a single theory, a single interpretation, or a single projection.

So the major issue in studying teaching is not the adoption of any single proposal, no matter how brilliant, but rather the inquiry and design of an integrated theory of teaching which recognizes existing models and is open, by its very structure, to any possible future expansion.

An integrated theory of teaching, as opposed to a mere smorgesbord of techniques, is necessary for three reasons: First, intellectual integrity calls for it; second, it provides a place for what has already been done; and third, it offers a place for the yet unknown.

An integrated theory of teaching provides for logical and reasonable mobility among universal alternatives without negating or destroying the idiosyncratic behavior which differentiates one teacher from another.

How well I remember the responses of many teachers in numerous workshops who feared to acknowledge, study, and experiment with alternatives. This fear, born of limitations, inevitably greets any new idea or proposal, the more so when the new proposal offers to dissect teaching behavior and to shake the very security of the teacher.

The Spectrum of Teaching Styles is an attempt to create an integrated theory of teaching which offers alternatives, mobility in relationships with students, and a wider range of security to both teacher and learner.

There are major problems confronting the designer of behavioral models. One, perhaps the foremost, is the need to reconcile a cool, logical, scientific approach to model-building with the not-so-cool, not-so-logical position of a humanist.

Proposed models for teaching behavior may approach the level of logical perfection. The human condition, inside and outside the classroom, does not. But it does not matter: Behavioral models can serve as guides that help us to identify our proximity to theoretically conceived arrangements and relationships.

The second major problem — and this one applies to every teacher — is the need to reconcile the emotional tensions, frustration, and recognition of inadequacy which confront almost anyone who attempts to use the entire Spectrum. Attempting to travel along the Spectrum always evokes these feelings. This is logical and understandable. Trying alternative behaviors calls for *introspection,* for self-knowledge and awareness of one's actions. This is often disturbing and occasionally distressing.

Try, then, any style that appeals to you. As you become comfortable in one, move to the next; select your order and sequence. When you have grappled with the frustrations and enjoyed the achievements of the entire Spectrum you will have reached the level of Teaching: From Command to Discovery.

Muska Mosston

Contents

1

The Genesis of the Spectrum of Teaching Styles

"Thou shalt teach them diligently unto thy children . . ."* is an edict of the ancient Hebrews, and so is it an edict of every social order. From early man's storytelling to the current sophisticated instruments for the collection, processing, and dissemination of information, man has been engaged in teaching. Everybody teaches. Everyone participates in this spectacular, complex, and mysterious activity. Mothers teach. Fathers teach. Children teach. Politicians teach. Policemen teach. Judges teach. Orchestra conductors teach. Military commanders teach. Artists teach. Writers teach. Philosophers teach. Movie stars teach. Shopkeepers teach. Lovers teach.

What is this phenomenon? What is this process that transcends time, distance, culture? What is it that we *do* when we teach? What is it that we *do not do?* What do we say? We have all experienced some joy in teaching. Why? We have all been angry—with ourselves, with the students, with the system. Why? The students we have taught have been joyous, upset, curious, angry, bored, excited, furious, delighted. Why?

Over the years many disciplines have offered answers to these questions, proposed ways to understand them. From philosophy and technology, from art and science have come insights, solutions, proposals, and models, as well as more questions and problems yet to be solved. Many disciplines have focussed on issues and forces which affect the act of teaching.

The question here, the most vital question, as far as teaching is concerned, is: how does all this vast accumulation of knowledge from so many disciplines affect teaching behavior? What does all this knowledge mean to the daily performance of a teacher in a classroom? How does a teacher internalize the statements of philosophers? How does the philosophy of a theoretician actually affect every act of the teaching

* Deuteronomy 6:7.

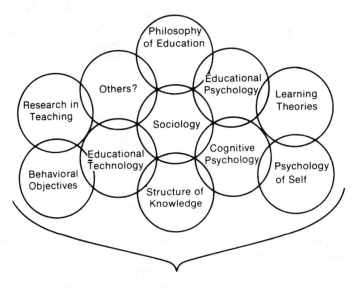

Teaching Behavior

experience? Should the nature of this relationship between theory and practice be left to the discretion or whim of the individual teacher?

How can a teacher assimilate the important yet terribly scattered information offered by educational psychology? For example, how can a teacher integrate into his teaching behavior the information about discrimination learning with and without errors and correction techniques offered by Terrace (45), Suppes and Ginsberg (42), or Bower (7)? Or, consider the controversy among educational psychologists over the issue of prompting in verbal instruction, prompting which is an important aspect of programmed instruction: one researcher, Cook (13), wrote "Superstition in the Skinnerian," and another, Holland (27), replied with "Cook's Tour de Farce." What is a teacher to do? Teachers hear a phrase like "learning sets," which was formulated by Harlow (26); but what does it mean to their behavior in the classroom? What about the issue of overt responses and reinforcement? Skinner (41) states: "Once we have arranged the particular type of consequence called a reinforcement, our techniques permit us to shape the behavior of an organism almost at will." Can a teacher shape the behavior of his students? What must the teacher do? What must he not do? *Should* he shape their behavior? Always? Never? Sometimes? These and myriad other issues and questions bombard the teacher who takes courses in educational psychology. They are important issues and the findings of educational psychology make an important contribution to the work of the teacher. But a serious difficulty arises in the all-too-common failure to employ these findings in the process of teaching teachers how to teach. One is reminded of the undergraduate who said, "My professor, while teaching us Skinnerian principles, was violating the very principles he was teaching." If the professor fails to employ the principles he is teaching, at least while that topic is under discussion, how can he expect the potential teacher to value those principles and to make use of them when he comes to teach his own subject?

Let us turn to the contribution of the humanist psychologists, whose works constantly alert us to the value of man as an organism that not only responds but, more importantly, has feelings about things, events, other people, and himself. Allport writes in his book *Becoming* (1):

> If the demand for autonomy were not a major force we could not explain the prominence of negativistic behavior in childhood. The crying, rejecting, and anger of a young infant as well as the negativistic behavior of the two-year-old are primitive indications of being bent on asserting itself. All his life long this being will be attempting to reconcile these two modes of becoming, the tribal and the personal: the one that makes him into a mirror, the other that lights the lamp of individuality within.

What does this need for self-assertion mean to teaching behavior? How can a teacher handle this dualism in the developing child? And what happens to the teacher's own need to become? How does the teacher handle his own "mirror" and "lamp" conflicts? Maslow (32) asserts that:

> The job of the psychotherapist (or the teacher) is to help a person find out what's already in him rather than to reinforce him or shape or teach him into a prearranged form, which someone else has decided upon in advance, a priori.

But how does a teacher *do* Maslow in chemistry, algebra, tumbling, shop, or music? How would a teacher confront the proposition made by Moustakas (36):

> Experience is true to the person when he is himself alone. In such experience perception is unique and undifferentiated. The individual is free to discover and express his potentialities. In true experience every expression is creative, the creation of the person one is and is becoming. There is only the exploring, spontaneously expressing self, finding satisfaction in personal being.

If a teacher identifies philosophically with this statement, how can he incorporate it into the act of teaching? What kind of teaching behavior will facilitate "true experience" in a given subject matter? What kind of teaching behavior will inhibit or abort "true experience"? Erving Goffman (23) in his book *Stigma* offers a striking description and analysis of what he characterizes as "stigmatizing" behavior and its effects on the feelings and behavior of the stigmatized person. A pluralistic society such as ours, one which is composed of a great variety of people, is susceptible to the stigma phenomenon. Our schools are populated with students who embody every conceivable human characteristic, all desires, aspirations, and forms of behavior—some concealed, some visible. What can a teacher do to discourage stigmatizing behavior in his students? What must a teacher do when faced with a student already affected by stigma? In a paper "Inclusion and Exclusion in Education," the author of this book (33) analyzes the relationships between educational practices and the process of exclusion. He asserts that the very design of the subject matter in many areas, the schools' environment and equipment, and the kinds of teaching behavior frequently demonstrated all result in exclusion. What kind of teaching behavior can minimize the exclusion of children who are different from the others, children who demonstrate different feelings, children who think differently, children who dare demonstrate a flare for the unusual? How must a teacher behave when confronted with children who cannot read, cannot speak well, cannot socialize, cannot express a thought, or cannot shoot a basket or hit a baseball?

Let us touch on a couple of other disciplines whose work relates to teaching behavior.

There is a magnificent wealth for the teacher in the efforts of cognitive psychologists. Their analyses of how man learns, how man thinks, how man solves, and how man creates offer abundant insights. But how can a teacher incorporate all this into action? What forms of teaching behavior would make use of Guilford's (24) proposals concerning the structure of the intellect? How can we design teaching models that put into effect the proposals made by Inhelder and Piaget (28), Bruner (11), Anderson and Ausubel (4), Gagné (20), Gage (19), Taba (43), Raths (38), Taylor (44), or Glaser (22)? In *Encouraging Creativity in the Classroom* Torrance (47) wrote:

> The past decade of educational research and development has brought increased recognition of the fact that man fundamentally prefers to learn in creative ways through creative and problem-solving activities. Teachers generally have insisted that it is more economical to learn by authority. It now seems that many important things, though not all, can be learned more effectively and economically in creative ways rather than by authority.

What, then, must teachers do—what is the teaching behavior that encourages creativity—by students, by teachers, by both?

Consider for a moment a sociologist's point of view; Melvin Tumin (48) in his article "Popular Culture and the Open Society" says:

Real creativity is viewed with suspicion and distrust because it means, above all, difference, intolerance, an insistence on achieving an individual identity. Real feeling is viewed with equal distrust and hostility because it almost always means bad manners, spontaneity, unpredictability, lack of realism, failure to observe routines.

Well-rounded, adjusted, happy—these are the things we are told it is important for us to be. No points, no sharp cutting edges, no despairs and elations. Just nice, smooth billiard balls, rolling gently on soft green cloth to our appointed, webbed pockets, and dropping slowly into the slots under the table to be used in the same meaningless way in the next game. Chalk up one for mediocrity. For it is the only winner in this game.

It seems that the teacher is constantly confronted with the "versus" issue—Skinner vs. Bruner, creativity vs. conformity, individualized instruction vs. group drills, flexible scheduling vs. traditional modes, media vs. man, the teacher's own idiosyncratic preferences vs. generalized models. Such opposing approaches do seem to represent something of a dilemma—an emotional, intellectual, and functional dilemma. But it is a meaningless dilemma—meaningless because man is not a one-dimensional creature and, therefore, no single plan, device, or form of teaching behavior can accommodate his full development.

The question is not Skinner vs. Bruner, creativity vs. conformity, and so on, along the path of opposing pairs; the question is *when* conformity? *when* creativity? *when* individualized instruction? *when* media? Every person, young or old, has experienced a multiplicity of learning and behaving styles. We have all responded to commands at times. The frequency and intensity of the response vary from person to person and from one time to another in the same person. We may like it or abhor it, but we have all experienced it. We have all had the experience of exercising individual initiative, when we have performed life tasks on our own. We have all solved problems large and small for ourselves: we have all participated in the joy of discovery. To deny man this multiplicity, to ignore this complexity is to fail to know man. To attempt to curb man's complexity is to diminish him.

Teaching therefore cannot be a one-dimensional form of behavior. The richer teacher is the one with the larger repertoire of behavioral models.

The Spectrum of Teaching Styles, the subject of this book, is a continuum of such models, models of teaching behavior. The continuum consists of an array of specific teaching styles, each of which can stand alone yet is integrally connected to the styles that precede and follow it on the continuum. Hence the concept of a spectrum of styles. The idea of a spectrum connotes cohesiveness among diverse elements. A spectrum of styles also suggests the possibility of development, of mobility and flexibility among those various styles. The idea of the spectrum emphasizes the *integration* of the various kinds of knowledge about teaching rather than their *fragmentation*. The spectrum identifies the place of a particular style within a larger context and clarifies its relationship to other styles. Such a construct helps us see both the particular style, its advantages and disadvantages, and the interdependency of styles within an integrated theory of teaching.

From command to discovery, the nickname of the spectrum, describes the range of possible teaching behavior encompassed on the spectrum; the phrase is also intended to suggest the dynamism of the spectrum, which does not prescribe any particular form of behavior but displays for the teacher the range of alternatives from which he can choose in any particular situation. The titles used in this book to distinguish the various styles are these: Command, Task, Reciprocal, Individual Program—Teacher's Design, Guided Discovery, Problem-Solving, and Individual Program—Student's Design. These teaching styles appear sequentially on the spectrum, each with its particular approach to the teaching-learning transaction, each with its peaks and pitfalls, each with its contributions and deterrents to physical development, social emancipation, and emotional maturity, as well as its impact on realizing the students' cognitive potentials.

The availability of related alternatives offers the teacher mobility and greater freedom. The teacher who is familiar with a variety of teaching styles is ready to cope with new conditions and to interact successfully with various forms of student behavior—to cope without threat, to experience without fear, and to bring to all his relations with students a contagious spirit of hope.

The detailed descriptions of each teaching style are intended to provide the teacher with an objective means of recognizing and analyzing the various styles. The spectrum seeks to provide the teacher with a rational basis for selecting a style appropriate to each particular group of students in each particular setting.

The first purpose of the spectrum is to make teachers more aware of their own teaching behavior. The power of the spectrum lies in the range of choices it provides for teachers. And the beauty of the spectrum is its ability to awaken teachers to their potential for reaching more students than is possible with a less comprehensive approach to teaching.

Every teacher has used one or more of these styles, perhaps all of them. Do teachers choose among them deliberately? Intuitively? By chance? Do teachers choose a particular style because they believe it to be their best one? Do they know about the others? Have they tried them? Frequently? How can teachers modify their styles to provide their students with the benefits implicit in styles other than their own? Or is a teacher locked into a given style of teaching because of his personality? Is personality a rigid, fixed entity?

The spectrum offers all teachers, preservice as well as experienced, the opportunity for introspection and growth. It is the purpose of this book not merely to persuade teachers to study the spectrum but to inspire them to *use* it and in doing so to exercise fully their own teaching abilities as they range from command to discovery.

2

The Anatomy of a Teaching Style

The Need for an Axiom

In searching for an axiom, a first statement, about *teaching behavior,* we are trying to identify *one statement* that is true and universal, and can therefore serve as the base for understanding and description that extend as far as our analytical powers allow. We are searching for the most fundamental possible descriptive statement that will embrace *all* teaching behavior.

If such an axiom can be identified, the foundation is laid for establishing a theoretical construct that will not only include the entire array of possible alternative models of teaching behavior but will also show the organic relationships among the different models. This should help guide the teacher in achieving *conscious* mobility from one behavioral model to the next. Thus perhaps the most painful problem in education can be alleviated: the problem of rigidity in teaching.

It is quite conceivable that a lack of flexibility in teaching behavior is due not only to philosophical fixation on a particular style of teaching, but also to *ignorance* of the existing alternatives and their implications. This ignorance about alternatives confirms teachers in doing what they have always done—teaching in a way that has "worked" for them, that has furnished a degree of daily security in the classroom, that has soothed their anxieties and provided a tolerable equilibrium with which to sustain the daily burdens and joys of their work.

But these are not quite adequate criteria. A theory of teaching that is highly operational cannot rely on random personal experiences, nor can it be built on an unrelated collection of gimmicks or principles or on scattered research finding. An integrated theory of teaching must offer an objective description so large in scope and so meticulous in its development that it will accommodate all existing and even all conceivable forms of teaching behavior, regardless of time, place, subject matter, *and* the personality of the teacher. Don't be alarmed. This is not an attempt to divest teaching of its humanity; on the contrary, it is an attempt to prevent the teachers' individual idiosyncrasies from becoming major educational tenets, rigid sets of principles, or even guiding philosophies which inhibit the growth of students.

An objective description of an integrated theory of teaching should clarify the differences between teaching styles and should sharpen the tools for observing teaching behavior and for perceiving those behavioral subtleties that teachers use to impose their personalities and viewpoints (regardless of their qualities) on their students. Such an objective description would not deny teachers their personalities and idiosyncrasies but would seek to *clarify* what teachers *do* and what they *do not do* during a particular teaching-learning transaction.

The Axiom

In this book we shall consider teaching behavior by the axiom that *teaching behavior is a chain of decision making.* This axiom suggests that everything the teacher does and says is a result of decisions previously made; every act, statement, or question of a teacher's is the consequence of such a decision. (We will discuss only conscious behavior; its unconscious and subconscious roots must be treated by the appropriate behavioral sciences.)

The statement that teaching behavior is a chain of decision making leads to the next imperative question: decisions about what?

In assembling and analyzing the available categories of decisions it has become evident that they all fall into three categories or sets of decisions that *must* be made whenever a teaching-learning transaction is in effect. The discussion here is not about *who* makes the given decision (this will come later) but rather about the decisions that must be made before, during, and after *any* transaction. No transaction can occur without these decisions. Even if a decision has not been made, regardless of reason, a decision was made *not* to make a decision.

Pre-Impact Decisions

The first set of decisions that *must* be made are identified as the *pre-impact* set. This set includes *all* the decisions that *must* be made *prior* to the encounter, before the impact of the meeting between teacher and student for any given event or episode. A delineation of the categories of decisions that *must* be made in the pre-impact set produces the following:

The Anatomy of a Style

Decision set	Decisions to be made

Pre-Impact
(content
preparation)
	1. whom to teach
	2. what to teach
	3. where to teach
	   a. starting
	   b. stopping
	   c. duration
	   d. rhythm/pace
	   e. interval
	   f. termination
	5. quality
	6. quantity
	7. communication
	8. teaching style
	9. anticipated learning style
	10. class climate
	11. why
	12. evaluative procedures and materials
	13. others

Impact (content execution: performance)	1. implementing and adhering to the set of pre-impact decisions 2. adjustment 3. others

Post-Impact
(content
evaluation)
	1. about feedback:
	   a. reinforcement: (1) immediate (2) delayed
	   b. correction: (1) immediate (2) delayed
	2. about interpreting and evaluative data procedures and materials
	   a. instrumentation
	   b. frequency
	   c. norms
	3. about the teaching-learning transaction itself
	4. others

1. Decisions about whom to teach   These are the decisions that are made concerning the participants in an episode. In any given class a teacher can address the entire class, part of it, or individuals. (This decision about whom to teach in a given class is separate from the institutional decision concerning who shall attend school.)

2. Decisions about what to teach   These pre-impact decisions pertain to subject matter. They are decisions about what to teach and what not to teach. Such decisions *must* be made. They also entail decisions about the structure of subject matter which in turn help shape the selection decisions. (A detailed, thorough treatment of the structure of subject matter appears in the discussion of the various styles of teaching.)

3. Decisions about where to teach   We can call these "geography" decisions. They come in many varieties: where to sit (or stand) in a classroom, where to be in a gymnasium, where to work in a laboratory, where to sit in a library, and so on. All geography decisions must be made in the pre-impact set.

4. Decisions about time   There are decisions about when to teach and decisions about when to make various decisions. There are "large" time decisions, which affect long-range curricula, and "smaller" time decisions, which concern only daily sessions. These latter are the minute decisions which determine *when to start* and *stop* a given activity: when to start reading the assignment in the class, when to start a particular movement in the gymnasium, when to start an experiment in the chemistry laboratory, and so on. "When to start" and "when to stop" decisions imply *duration decisions,* about the elapsed time between the beginning and the end of an activity. Intrinsic to time decisions are *pace and rhythm decisions* (no activity occurs in zero time, without pace or rhythm). There is also a kind of time decision we can call *interval decisions,* which affect the learner's experience during the period between a "stop" decision and the next "start" decision. Finally, there is the *termination decision,* a decision *not* to devote any more time (currently or in the future) to the larger set of experiences: the reading assignment, the lab experiment, etc. Time decisions *must* be made.

7. Decisions about quantity   These are decisions about "how much" is to be done, experienced, or learned. Certain school subjects lend themselves more readily to this kind of decision than do others. In music a decision can be made to repeat the playing of a given violin concerto or parts of it so many times; in physical education a decision can be made about the quantity of a given movement experience — running a mile, or a half-mile, or a quarter-mile. Writing a given word fifty times in spelling or thinking through a given concept in physics (e.g., the laws governing falling bodies) does not quite provide for this kind of a quantitative decision.

6. Decisions about quality   These are decisions about "how well" the students are to perform, perceive, learn, execute, or present the subject matter. Here too there are either inherent limitations which are affected by the kind of subject matter, its structure, and our methods for assessing quality, or those limitations imposed by cultural selectivity and personal points of view. In any case, quality decisions *must* be made.

7. Decisions about the style to be used   These are decisions strongly affecting teaching behavior. Assuming that the teacher is familiar with and versed in alternative styles of teaching and is aware of the various implications of *each* style, then it *must* be decided which style of teaching is to be used in a particular situation, with particular students, in a particular subject. (The integration of a teaching style with the structure of subject matter and its relationship to learning will be given detailed analysis in the discussion of the various teaching styles.)

8. Decisions about the anticipated learning style   Since people learn in different ways and employ a variety of cognitive behaviors while they learn, it is necessary to anticipate (or recognize) the kind of learning students demonstrate. Thus, the teacher's desire for a particular learning style influences the selection of a teaching style and, conversely, the use of a particular teaching style should elicit a particular learning style.

9. Decisions about class climate   These are certain decisions about the social-emotional climate of the classroom. Some might call them *discipline decisions.* They are intimately related to the decision about teaching style because each style affects the social-emotional tone of teacher-student and student-student relationships in its own particular way. Different teaching styles help create different classroom climates, and, conversely, differences in the social-emotional climate of the classroom affect the choice of teaching style. These kinds of decisions are analyzed in detail in the discussions of each of the various teaching styles.

10. Decisions about communication   (See: classroom communication model in Chapter 4.) This involves decisions about choice of words, form of speech, and use of media.

11. Decisions about why   These decisions represent a philosophy of education, a set of values, a point of view.

12. Decisions about evaluative procedures and materials   These decisions affect the evaluation behavior, the techniques, the testing materials to be employed in the post-impact set.

13. Others?   Perhaps there are other kinds of decisions that must be made in the pre-impact set. Can you offer any? The set is open-ended.

The pre-impact set of decisions applies to *all* teaching situations. Even if some of the decisions (or theoretically, all the decisions), for whatever reason, have not been made, a *decision* was made *not* to make these decisions. It is imperative to keep in mind the openness and fluidity of the pre-impact set, so that any additional categorical decisions discovered can be inserted into this schema.

Impact Decisions

The second set of decisions that must be made is the *impact* set. It includes *all* the decisions that must be made *during* the teaching-learning transaction. The *content* of the decisions in the pre-impact set is planning and preparation; the *content* of the decisions in the impact set is execution and performance. These execution decisions demonstrate the consequences of the pre-impact decisions. These are decisions made *during the transaction.*

1. Decisions about whom to teach   During the teaching-learning process these kinds of decisions must be made about the following considerations:

    a.   With whom to speak when there is more than one person.
    b.   Whom to hear at a particular time.
    c.   At whom to look.
    d.   Whom to touch.
    e.   Other?

These are some of the ways in which teachers communicate with their students, often without consciously deciding to do so. But the important point here is that *conscious decisions* about these facets of communication can enrich the relationship between teacher and student and thus enhance the learning process. Awareness of such decisions also prepares the teacher for deciding what *not* to do, at whom *not* to look, to whom *not* to talk, and whom *not* to hear or touch.

2. Decisions about what to teach   These are decisions which must be made in order to implement the pre-impact decisions about what to teach:

Initiation decision   What is the very first step in initiating the subject to be taught? What do you actually *do?* What *don't* you do? Why? These questions apply not only to large segments of the curriculum, but also and continuously to every act of teaching, every day, in every subject.

Teacher's verbal behavior decisions   The words uttered during the transaction affect what is taught and what is learned. Decisions about the teacher's verbal behavior are intrinsically and powerfully connected with the *initiation decisions,* because the first words, the first phrases used often determine the intensity of contact between teacher and student. Verbal behavior is discussed in subsequent chapters in connection with each style, as its effects vary from style to style.

3. Decisions about where to teach   These decisions implement the pre-impact "geography" decisions. They reflect the teacher's sensitivity to the comfort and convenience of the classroom, both for himself and for his students. These decisions raise questions about hearing, seeing, comfortable posture, and convenience of the area in the performance of any activity required by the subject matter. These are, in effect, organizational decisions which change from one style of teaching to another.

4. Decisions about time   The various aspects of time that were considered in the pre-impact set reappear here as execution decisions about: (a) starting; (b) stopping; (c) pace and rhythm; (d) interval; (e) termination; (f) other?

5. Decisions about quantity   These decisions implement the pre-impact quantity decisions, which had to do with "how much" of a particular subject students should be expected to learn.

6. Decisions about quality   Quality decisions have to be made *during* the impact set; these decisions will vary with the different teaching styles.

7. Decisions about the choice of teaching style   Executing the teaching style chosen in the pre-impact set will affect how each of the other pre-impact decisions (how, what, to whom, etc.) is executed. Full adherence to the chosen teaching style is not intended to produce rigid behavior, but rather to enable observation of how closely practice can approximate a meticulous theoretical model. (See 10, below.)

8. Decisions about the anticipated learning style   Adherence to the chosen teaching style during the impact set creates clearer possibilities for the occurrence of a given learning style (including its individual variations) which closely corresponds to the selected teaching style.

9. Decisions about classroom climate   To the extent that the previous eight categories of decisions faithfully execute the pre-impact decisions, the classroom climate will be predictable.

10. Adjustment decisions   These decisions are perhaps the most useful in the impact set, but they are also the most subtle. They are subtle because they require an awareness of the differences between pre-impact and impact decisions. They are useful because they dictate alterations in the decisions made and the decisions to be made.

In most, if not all, actual teaching situations there will be many discrepancies between the two sets of decisions. There are often, perhaps always, factors that interfere with the smooth flow of the impact set of decisions. These must be considered as *intervening variables* and must be treated as they arise. When an intervening variable affects the smooth flow of decision execution, an *adjustment decision* must be made so that the process continues. Adjustment decisions vary in content:

a.   They can *alter* action that follows from an earlier decision.
b.   They can *stop* action that is already in process as the result of an earlier decision.
c.   They can *ignore* an earlier decision and thus prevent whatever action would have followed from it.

Adjustment decisions can alter, stop, or ignore *any* of the decisions of the impact set *during* the teaching-learning process, and they can alter, stop, or ignore any of the pre-impact set *before* the teaching-learning process begins. Adjustment decisions are one kind of post-impact decision that are made after an episode within the impact set and are applied *during* that impact set. They are adjustments made to the execution of the style. Adjustment decisions can thus affect any decision in the first two sets.

Teachers will need to become quite skillful in making and executing adjustment decisions because they vary in kind and manner from style to style. An inappropriate adjustment decision can cancel the advantages of a teaching style and thus neutralize the anticipated learning style. This often happens to a teacher who is a novice in the use of a particular style. When something unexpected happens, the tendency of the novice teacher is to abandon the new style and retreat to a more familiar style, one that feels safer to him. It may not be more appropriate and safe for the students but it seems to help reestablish the security of the teacher. With this decision to retreat, the teacher of course loses whatever advantages he had originally sought in the new style. But as he increases his understanding of the theoretical structure of each style and as he gains experience in using it, the teacher will become more adept at making adjustment decisions without retreating to another style.

Schematically, the potential effect of the adjustment looks like this:

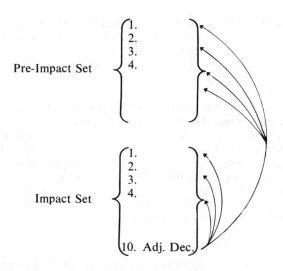

Pre-Impact Set
1.
2.
3.
4.

Impact Set
1.
2.
3.
4.

10. Adj. Dec.

11. Other decisions that affect the impact?

Post-Impact Decisions

The third set of decisions that must be made is the post-impact set. These are all the *evaluation decisions* that are made after the impact occurs. In the course of any teaching-learning transaction, evaluation decisions are constantly made. They may or may not be overt, but they are there. The slightest grimace in response to something said or done, the least thought about the performance of a task—these represent evaluation decisions. Even if (theoretically) no evaluation decision has been made, a *decision* was made *not* to make a decision. Here is a list of some of the categories of evaluation decisions:

1. Decisions which represent immediate feedback procedures. (The vast psychological literature on immediate knowledge of results and its effect on learning is readily available.)
2. Decisions about reinforcement in general.
3. Decisions about specific kinds of reinforcement following the performance of specific tasks.
4. Decisions about daily evaluations:
    a. *procedures:* These decisions concern the methods of gathering data about the student: tests, rating scales, profile charts, interaction-analysis techniques, audio tape recordings, video tape recordings, and so on.

    b. *frequency:* These are decisions about how often these data-gathering procedures are utilized. This includes the rationale supporting the frequency selected.

    c. *norms:* These are decisions about the use of norms when interpreting the gathered data for determining the student's standing in the class.

5. Decisions about the teaching-learning transaction itself. These are the decisions about the effectiveness of a particular style in a particular classroom session. The details of this evaluation process are offered in discussions of the "implication of the style" in each chapter.

6. Reward and reprimand decisions. The reward and reprimand system used in a particular situation depends on the style of teaching employed. The description and analysis of each style of teaching will include a discussion of the kind of reward and reprimand system which is intrinsic to the structure of that style.

These three sets of decisions combine to form the Anatomy of a Teaching Style. This arrangement serves as the cornerstone of the Spectrum of Teaching Styles. Perhaps the most powerful value of the Anatomy of a Teaching Style is its universality. Any teaching-learning situation in any subject matter involves all of these decisions—indeed, categorically—all these decisions must be made in any teaching-learning transaction. Differing conditions may affect quantity, quality, frequency, intensity, and level of these decisions but they are all *intrinsic* to any teaching act.

Again, the schema of the Anatomy is:

The Anatomy of a Style

Decision set	Decisions to be made

Pre-Impact (content preparation)	1. whom to teach
	2. what to teach
	3. where to teach
	4. time
	   a. starting
	   b. stopping
	   c. duration
	   d. rhythm/pace
	   e. interval
	   f. termination
	5. quality
	6. quantity
	7. communication
	8. teaching style
	9. anticipated learning style
	10. class climate

	11. why
	12. evaluative procedures and materials
	13. others
Impact (content execution: performance)	1. implementing and adhering to the set of pre- impact decisions 2. adjustment 3. others

Post-Impact
(content
evaluation)
	1. about feedback:
	  a. reinforcement: (1) immediate (2) delayed
	  b. correction: (1) immediate (2) delayed
	2. about interpreting and evaluative data procedures
	  and materials
	  a. instrumentation
	  b. frequency
	  c. norms
	3. about the teaching-learning transaction itself
	4. others

3

Emergence of the Command Style

The Anatomy of a Teaching Style provides a generalized overview of those decisions that must be made before, during, and after every teaching-learning transaction. It does not, however, show a *particular* style of teaching. Therefore, several questions arise at this point in the evolution of the Spectrum:

1. How can the Anatomy of a Style be used to identify and delineate a *particular* style of teaching? What must be done with it to evolve a given, identifiable style?
2. According to this anatomy, is there only *one* style of teaching? If so, then: What is it? What does it look like?
3. If not, if there is *more* than one style, then: What are they? How many are there?
4. If there is more than one style, how do any two styles differ?
5. Assuming a multiplicity of styles (all emerging and evolving from the Anatomy of a Style), how are they related? Is there an intrinsic organization which binds them together? Are they randomly scattered?

Perhaps the most perplexing question is: where do we begin? Is there a first style?—a first step toward the evolution of an integrated theory of teaching that can be both descriptive and prescriptive?

By superimposing the "Theoretical Limits" concept on the anatomy of a style it becomes possible to establish at least one of the polarities of the theoretical limits continuum.

The theoretical limits concept is of a continuum that extends from minimum to maximum. Minimum and maximum on the theoretical limits refer to the proportion of decisions made by the participants in the transaction. What relationship exists or might exist between this kind of a continuum and the Anatomy, the three sets of decisions?

Since the transaction is between teacher and student, the question is what would a style of teaching be like if we tried, for example, to identify

The Anatomy of a Style

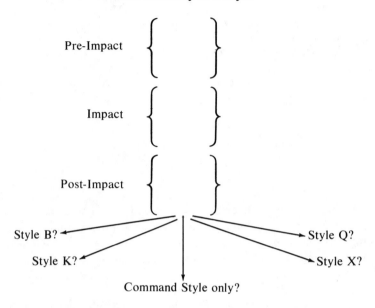

Pre-Impact

Impact

Post-Impact

Style B? ←   → Style Q?

Style K? ←   → Style X?

Command Style only?

Styles randomly scattered?

or

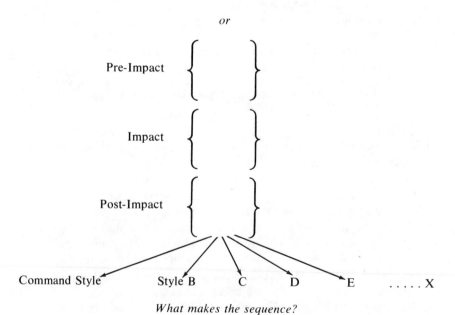

Pre-Impact

Impact

Post-Impact

Command Style   Style B   C   D   E   X

What makes the sequence?

Theoretical Limits Concept

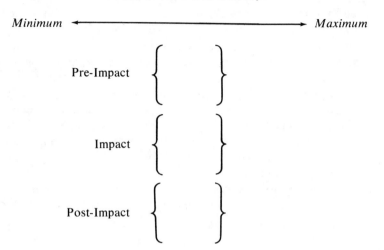

What are the possible relationships?

Command Style Teaching Profile

	Teacher		Student	
Decision to be made	*Yes*	*No*	*Yes*	*No*
	√		√	
	√		√	
	√		√	
	√		√	
	√		√	
	√		√	
	√		√	
	√		√	
	√		√	
	√		√	
	√		√	
	√		√	
	√		√	
	√		√	
	√		√	
	√		√	
	√		√	
	√		√	
	√		√	
	√		√	
	√		√	

the possible relationships between the maximum on the limits continuum and the teacher, through the Anatomy of a Style. Theoretically, it would mean that the teacher would make *all* the decisions in *all* three sets. If the teacher makes *all* the decisions, theoretically the student makes none; the role of the student is to obey, respond, perform, and follow.

The checks represent only categorical decisions. A fully delineated decisions list for any given lesson on any subject matter will include a great number of decisions in each set, but the general appearance of the Teaching Profile will be the same since it records all decisions made by the teacher as described and prescribed by the theoretical structure of this style, the Command Style.

It is interesting to observe a teacher attempting to *simulate* this teaching behavior model. Consider making *all* the conceivable decisions

The Anatomy of the Command Style

Decision sets	Decisions made by the teacher	Decisions by student
Pre-Impact	1. Whom to teach	not involved
	2. What to teach	not involved
	3. Where to teach	not involved
	4. Time	not involved
	5. Quantity	not involved
	6. Quality	not involved
	7. Teaching-learning transaction	not involved
	8. Anticipated learning style	not involved
	9. Class climate	not involved
	10. Communication	not involved
	11. Why	not involved
	12. Evaluative procedures	not involved
	13. Other	not involved
Impact	1–10. Implementation decisions	Student responds as prescribed
	11. Adjustment decisions	not involved
	12. Other?	not involved
Post-Impact	1. Feedback	not involved
	2. Reinforcement	not involved
	3. Corrections	not involved
	4. Evaluation:	
	a. Procedures	not involved
	b. Frequency	not involved
	c. Norms	not involved
	5. Teaching-learning transaction	not involved

in the anatomy of this style using any phase of *your* subject matter. Could you behave like this?

Let's look at some examples in various subjects. Let's see what the use of this style means in different instances. We will proceed objectively by following the descriptive analysis of the decisions that must be made. We will refrain from value judgments for the time being. Let us find out as much as we can about the theoretical design of this style and its *application* to various subjects.

As we attempt to behave according to this style to approximate its theoretical model, the pure and perfect form of the style, we develop insights into the *assets* and *liabilities* of the style. We become aware of what a given style of teaching does *to* people, *for* people, or *against* people. This kind of observation provides for a rather thorough analysis of the *implications* of each style of teaching for any and all facets of the educational experience.

So there are four steps to becoming acquainted with the Spectrum of Teaching Styles:

1. Knowing the theoretical structure of each style.
2. Applying the theoretical structure to reality in your subject matter — acquiring the behavior of each style.
3. Understanding the implications of your behavior in each style.
4. Choosing the styles you prefer to use under different conditions.

Step four cannot be taken until the first three have been taken.

Now back to the application of the Command Style. Let us examine the operation of this style in teaching *spelling*. In order to adhere to the dictum of the Command Style, all decisions concerning *every* aspect of spelling must be made by the teacher.

Spelling can be learned by several different combinations of perceptual input mechanisms:

a. Seeing the spelling and then saying it.
b. Hearing the spelling and then saying it.
c. Seeing the spelling and then writing it.
d. Hearing the spelling and then writing it.
e. Other.

For our example here we'll use hearing the spelling and then writing it.

Let us focus on the impact set of decisions. We should be able to highlight the relationship between the theoretical model of the Command Style and its application in action. Clearly, in this style a teacher can decide to do almost anything in the pre-impact set.

Command Style Impact-Set *Category of decisions*	*Subject: Spelling* *Mode: Hearing the spelling* *and then writing it* *Specific decisions made by the teacher*
1. Decisions about whom to teach.	a. Every student in the class. b. Communication will be done with the entire class at the same time. c. Communication will be done with one at a time.

2. Decisions about what to teach.	a. The spelling of the word *spectrum* will be taught (assuming the students know the letters). (One word only was selected so that we can concentrate on the process under discussion.)
	b. *Initiation decision:* The teacher sounds the word *spectrum*.
	c. The teacher sounds every letter separately. This requires additional decisions about:
	  i. the volume of sound;
	  ii. the length of the interval between the sounding of each letter;
	  iii. the length of time used to sound each letter;
	  iv. the number of repetitions of the sounding of each letter;
	  v. which sounds need not be repeated;
	  vi. other?
	  (The intention here is not to be microscopic to the point of absurdity, but to show the intrinsic relationship between decision-making and the very particular aspects of teaching a subject. Again, the Command Style requires that *all* these decisions be made by the teacher. The teacher cannot arbitrarily skip or ignore any of these decisions. If he does, he will no longer approximate the theoretical model of the Command Style; it will be something else.)

3. Decisions about where to teach.	a. Each student sits in his chair. b. The teacher stipulates a specific posture for the students. c. The teacher tells the students how to hold the pencil, where to place the notebook, etc.

Command Style Impact-Set Category of decisions	Subject Spelling Mode: Hearing the spelling and then writing it Specific decisions made by the teacher
4. Decisions about time.	a. The teacher decides when to start the sounding of the word *spectrum*. b. How long will the sounding of the word last? c. Do the students begin to write while the teacher is still sounding the word? Or at the instant of its completion? Or at a special signal to start writing? d. Writing duration: How much time is allotted for the writing of each letter? e. Interval decision: How long does the teacher pause between calling out the letters?
5. Decisions about quantity.	a. The teacher decides how many times the students will write the word *spectrum*.
6. Decisions about quality.	a. First the teacher must decide what standards he will use in judging the quality of the students' work. Standards vary, and it is up to the teacher to set his own standards in the subject at hand. b. The teacher must decide how to convey his quality standards to the students. Besides determining how many spelling mistakes to allow, the teacher may decide to judge quality according to the *size* of the students' written letters and the *distance* between letters. And perhaps there will be other aspects of students' handwriting that will help determine quality. However the teacher decides to judge quality, it is important that the students know what the teacher expects of them.
7. Decisions about teaching style.	a. The teacher decides to maintain the Command Style during the entire process of teaching the spelling of the word *spectrum*. Perhaps it is relevant to say that it is, indeed, difficult in the beginning

Command Style Impact-Set Category of decisions	Subject: Spelling Mode: Hearing the spelling and then writing it Specific decisions made by the teacher
	to sustain the teaching behavior of any style. It is not even suggested that one must sustain a given style during an entire session. It is important, however, to experiment with one's teaching behavior and *insist* on several experiences in sustaining each style for several complete teaching experiences. This provides the teacher with a great deal of information about the operational level of a style, about the way students learn by a given style, and about *himself;* about the meaning of a given style and how it relates to the teacher's needs, personality, and aspirations.
8. Decisions about the anticipated learning style.	a. A decision that the student will produce given responses when given stimuli are emitted. b. Decision to sustain the S − R relationship as the learning style for this session.
9. Decisions about classroom climate.	a. Decision about the group readiness to receive the stimulus: to hear the called-out word. b. Decision that there will be no deviation from the procedures established by previous decisions. c. Members of the class are expected to produce the responses as prescribed.
10. Adjustment decisions.	a. As needed.

So, simulating the Command Style seems to induce decisions and awareness of details which otherwise go unnoticed.

This behavior requires considerable insight into the components of the given activity or experience.

Now, an earlier statement that *all* decisions in this style are made by the teacher and that the student makes no decision needs to be reexamined, because although theoretically it may be a true statement, operationally it is not so. The student *always* has the opportunity to say no. (Man has this unique ability to refuse. Some men have chosen death rather than obey the commands of others.)

A student has the intrinsic ability (we are not talking about right!) to make *one* decision of *not* responding to one, any, or all the decisions made by the teacher. Schematically:

	teacher decides	*student decides*
theoretically	all	none
operationally	all − 1	1 (yes or no)

Here are some guidelines to consider when preparing sessions in various subjects to be taught by this style. In social studies, for example, when teaching about social revolution the Command Style *requires* that the teacher will do the following:

1. Explain what a social revolution is.
2. Give one actual revolution as an example.
3. Show how this revolution illustrates the general definition.
4. Analyze the advantages (if any, by the teacher's criteria) of the particular revolution.
5. Analyze its disadvantages (if any).
6. Select the written data that support the point of view (books, pamphlets, etc.).
7. Select the visual data which support the point of view (films, news clips, etc.).
8. Supply witnesses to enhance the presented point of view (people who participated in that revolution and hold the point of view presented).
9. Make sure that *no choice-materials* are available to the students, because these might lead students to a point of view other than the one presented. This violates the intent and procedures of the Command Style.
10. Prepare and administer tests and materials which evaluate the student's grasp of the materials and point of view presented.
11. Assess the *success* or *failure* of the student according to the test results. Success would mean the student could reproduce the information presented, failure would mean he could not.
12. Prevent (by any means?) any student from presenting to the class materials or a point of view other than the one presented. Again, this activity would violate the Command Style because the student presenting the materials would have made decisions about subject matter.

It must be understood that the Command Style of teaching behavior *does not* prevent alternatives, only those offered by others; alternatives the teacher has chosen become legitimate.

This sample of one session in one topic in social studies can, of course, be extended to many other topics in this field and can be extended over weeks, a semester, a year, or over the entire career of a given teacher.

In physical education, the Command Style would mean that the teacher makes all the decisions about class organization in the gym, the specific posture and exercises for all students, the standard of performance, the rate of performance, the aesthetic standard of performance, the performance hierarchy in the class, the specific rules for any activity and performance, and, indeed, decisions about many other aspects of the student's life in and out of the gym.

A good part of the subject matter of physical education lends itself to these kinds of decisions, and the high *visibility* of activity provides an immediate way to check the responses to the teacher's decisions. About the uses and abuses of this style in physical education, see the author's "Inclusion and Exclusion in Physical Education" (33) and "Mission, Omission and Submission in Physical Education," (34) by the author and Mueller.

In art education it would mean that the teacher makes decisions about:

1. What is to be painted, drawn, sculpted, photographed, and so on.
2. The materials to be used, both in general and for the particular project at hand.
3. Tools to be used.
4. Colors to be used.
5. The size of the art product.
6. The amount and consistency of the paint.
7. The kind of strokes used in a painting.
8. The color combinations.
9. The perspective used.
10. Keeping or eliminating parts of the painting which are not "right."
11. The interpretation of the student's art product.
12. Interpretation by comparison against other student's products or a standard chosen by the teacher.
13. Other.

Carrying the Command Style to its logical limits in an art class would also mean that the teacher makes decisions about:

1. The posture while drawing.
2. How the brush and other tools are held.

3. How the apron is put on.
4. How hands are washed.
5. How the paper is folded or rolled.
6. How the art product is displayed.
7. Other.

In mathematics — no matter what the topic or concept in a given lesson — the teacher will make decisions about:

1. Selecting the topic for a particular lesson.
2. Stating the topic, principle, formula, and so on.
3. Identifying the premise or assumption that is required in the development of the topic.
4. Applying one or a series of statements that show the development of the topic.
5. Developing the steps in the formulation of these statements.
6. Arranging the sequence of these steps.
7. Reaching a single or multiple solution.
8. Stating the solution (orally and/or in writing).
9. Preparing test questions on the material, its development, and its solution.
10. Other.

The powerful, precise logic of mathematics lends itself to this kind of teaching behavior. The inherent truth in much of mathematics seems to have given strong support to the frequent use of this style by math teachers, both before and since the introduction of the "new math" to the schools.

The Role of Demonstration

One of the powerful techniques used in the Command and other styles is the demonstration. *All* media are used for demonstrations. Demonstration has been used to convey information in almost every subject as well as in most areas of experience outside the school. For example:

The mathematics teacher demonstrates how to solve a problem in algebra.
The music teacher demonstrates a passage in a piano concerto by playing it.
The art teacher demonstrates strokes with a brush to produce a particular image.
The physical education teacher demonstrates the handstand by doing it.
The social studies teacher demonstrates an analysis of a social event by doing it.
The shop teacher demonstrates the use of a tool.

The language teacher demonstrates by talking to the class in that particular language.

The literature teacher demonstrates by reciting and analyzing a poem.

A salesman demonstrates his goods by displaying them.

A play, a number, or a theatre piece demonstrate an idea, a point of view, a story.

A clergyman demonstrates objects and procedures. It is called *performing the ritual.*

The president demonstrates his point of view by analysis of the situation and plans. It is sometimes called delivering the state of the Union.

Demonstrations, since they use all modes of communication, can be involved in any and all components of any communication set, for any content, mode, action, medium, direction, and time.

Characteristics of a Demonstration

A demonstration is an illustrative performance of a complete event or part of it, showing also the interrelationships among its component parts and, if the subject of the demonstration is a procedure, the proper chronological sequence among the related parts. If a procedure or process is being demonstrated — whether an algebra problem, or setting the timing of an automobile's distributor, or, witnessed through a microscope, meiosis — then its initiation, all steps in the process, and its termination and the final product will have been demonstrated.

Of course, by the demonstration of a procedure a standard of performance will have been established — perhaps even, implicitly or explicitly, barring any alternative procedures as inferior or incorrect. This will encourage some witnesses of the demonstration and discourage others, perhaps, according to their attitudes towards the standards and their expectations about the likelihood of meeting them. The difference in the skill of the demonstrator and that of the witnesses will have the same effect. And demonstration of a procedure, even if it is not claimed to be the only way, will discourage experimentation in thought or behavior by favoring imitation. If different ways of thinking are thereby discouraged, so then are different evaluative procedures, and, hence, the "truth" of the content cannot be examined.

Assets and Liabilities of the Command Style

Before we go on to discuss the implications of the Command Style, let us see what it *does* and *does not do.*

What does the Command Style do?	*What does the Command Style not do?*
1. Establishes clear objectives to be reached by all students.	1. Does not consider the objectives of the individual (the student).
2. Develops externally observable group discipline.	2. Does not admit a wider definition of discipline: inner, self-discipline.
3. Distinguishes the "deviants," those who cannot reach the standard.	3. Does not admit differences in cultural or innate abilities.
4. Establishes the teacher as the sole decision maker about subject, organization, discipline, standards, and the like.	4. Does not allow any decisions by the student, and thus aborts the potential of the emerging self.
5. Recognizes only alternatives designed by the teacher.	5. Does not recognize alternatives designed by students.
6. Establishes student hierarchy determined by the best possible procedures of evaluation compatible only with this style of teaching.	6. Does not recognize alternative, multiple hierarchies of students based on alternative evaluations.
7. Reflects the philosophy that there is only one set of educational goals.	7. Does not recognize the uniqueness of the individual as the focus of education.
8. Upholds the concept of fixed intelligence.	8. Does not question its own assets, and rarely (if ever) identifies its liabilities.
9. Denies differences in individual abilities, interests, and aspirations.	9. Others?
10. Other?	

From such observations, this style has been called by a variety of names: autocratic, dictatorial, teacher-centered, military, and the like.

Implications of the Command Style

Let's begin with a schematic arrangement which will identify the relationship between the Command Style and various activities, processes, and criteria.

The Command Style and Philosophy of Education

There is no need here to expound on how a philosophy of education develops purposes, social goals, and guides for a working theory and applications for schools. The problem never lies in the stated philosophy,

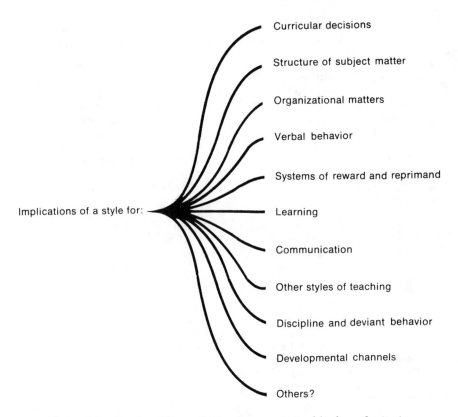

Implications of a style for:

- Curricular decisions
- Structure of subject matter
- Organizational matters
- Verbal behavior
- Systems of reward and reprimand
- Learning
- Communication
- Other styles of teaching
- Discipline and deviant behavior
- Developmental channels
- Others?

Chart of Implication. *The activities, processes, and bodies of criteria or interrelationships that the Command Style affects are schematically indicated by connecting lines. These same connections will hold for any teaching style on the Spectrum.*

but in its translation into daily classroom practices. American educational literature abounds with data on the breakdown between the two, philosophy and behavior. Certainly for more than half a century almost every book on education or teaching contains a banner chapter on democracy and its fundamental principles: respect for the individual, recognition of differences among individuals, promulgation of basic freedoms, and the like. In general, the tenets and spirit of American education proclaim that the rights of man are to enable him to be, to become. But the political realities of the sixties and the early seventies provide evidence to the contrary.

What does all this have to do with teaching behavior, and with the Command Style in particular? The full and accurate implementation of a philosophy of education can be accomplished, or aborted, only in the daily behavior of each teacher in every classroom.

Teachers who persistently use the Command Style imply that they believe that decision distribution must follow a hierarchy: from the top down, from the teacher to the student. Whatever the merits or hazards of this kind of a relationship, persistent use of the Command Style reflects a philosophy of constant, centralized control, and one rigid set of uniform behavioral standards applied to all. Some societies state that this *is* their point of view, their way of life; and their teachers behave accordingly. However, it is quite incongruent to observe teachers in American schools who, before your eyes, execute the Command Style in detail while concurrently spouting paeans to student freedom and studding the preamble to nearly every school curricular guide in the country with statements in favor of individual creativity. Our argument is not with the teacher's philosophy, but with the teacher's blindness.

When all decisions are made by the teacher, there can be no development of democratic procedures, and certainly no experience by the student of a freeing process that would maximize the individual's freedom and uniqueness. The Command Style and these goals are mutually exclusive.

If a school board were to announce publicly that a given school program is designed for conformity, rigidity, and total obedience to decisions made by others, then the Command Style of teaching, in all subjects and at all times, would be most appropriate; the teaching style totally congruent with the stated philosophy.

The Command Style and Curricular Decisions

Use of the Command Style, then, has many implications for curricular design, content, and direction. The Command Style is not confined only to teachers – some principals and superintendents share it. So, in a school where the Command Style is the modus operandi the curriculum will be rather stable and steady (perhaps even antiquated). It will contain "standard" subjects and "standard" materials for these subjects. Procedures for learning conduct will be clear and specified, and levels of expectation known to all. Curricular reviews will occur by *decree,* not by *need;* curricular changes by *command,* not by *choice.*

The most interesting facet of such an arrangement is *obedient behavior.* It is the belief or the pretense that the one on top knows more and better; that the one below must accept, obey, and follow; that one must not doubt, question, or change.

The Command Style and the Structure of Subject Matter

In decisions about the structure of subject matter the use of the Command Style produces intellectual oppression. Since the teacher makes decisions about everything, those made about subject matter must project the *truth;* hence, whatever the teacher says—about *anything*—must be accepted. The Command Style of teaching has evolved sets of "rights" and "wrongs" (official truths) in practically every subject matter in any curriculum (including the sciences, which are presumably objective). These are not *intrinsically* "rights" and "wrongs," but are so because of the value system reflected by the Command Style. "Rights" and "wrongs" are peculiar to the Command Style because they are dictated by authority. Behavior on this premise occurs daily in our schools when teachers make decisions about facts, principles, relationships, concepts, conclusions—all presented to the student as *truths* to be accepted, remembered, and used.

In addition to the danger it poses to political and social freedom, this behavior denies the very ability of the intellect to seek and test alternative ideas, principles, and conclusions. Given free scope, the ever-vibrant cognitive processes constantly produce questions, challenge the status quo, create alternatives, but the Command Style is designed to subdue all these through the narrow presentation of subject matter and the dogmatic transmission of human knowledge: cognitive submission to restricted and selected truth. (A thinking exercise for the reader: Can you identify *one instance* in the following subjects which has been presented to students by command, has served as an unshakeable truth and a "must" in the program, and somehow, after some time, has ceased to be true and has been dropped from the program? Try to locate this example in: American history, physics, physical education, health science, or any other subject.)

It must be said, though, that there are activities and parts of subjects that *intrinsically require* the Command Style of teaching and learning, and its equivalent for behavior in general. That is, any other conduct will endanger either the integrity of the subject matter or the safety of the participants. Examples:

1. When a traffic light turns red (the stimulus), you stop (the response): Any possible alternative is not feasible or desirable.
2. In a military marching drill, when the officer delivers the command, *all* participants must respond in all specifications. The command (stimulus) *atten-tion!* requires all to assume a specific posture (response)—*now!*
3. In music, performance of a symphony makes it imperative that the players respond most precisely to the commands of the conductor in beat, tempo, loudness, intervals, and so on. This will maintain the in-

tegrity of the symphony. (On the other hand, the conductor can only execute the instructions of the composer with latitude of interpretation if the separate integrities of the composer and the conductor are to be maintained: Toscanini, when accused by his players of being a tyrant, replied: "Democracy in politics—in music, aristocracy!")

4. Can you think of other examples?

The Command Style and Other Styles of Teaching

For treatment of this, let's develop the Spectrum and the evolution of other styles of teaching further.

The Command Style and Communication

Here again, let us wait for a fuller discussion of verbal communication and demonstration, in the next chapter, on the Task Style.

Implications of Command Style for Discipline and Deviant Behavior

Discipline traditionally means doing things *as prescribed;* deviant behavior means doing things in *other* than prescribed ways. The Command Style demands discipline, and since the style governs all aspects of behavior in the classroom, it follows that this style can have only two kinds of consequences:

1. Students who conform to discipline; who do as prescribed.
2. Deviants of various kinds; students who *cannot* or *will not* do as prescribed.

Let's talk about the second group. The meaning, procedures, and consequences of the first are quite clear.

People who *cannot* are those who have one or more personal limitations: perceptual; physical; intellectual; linguistic; cultural; economic; or others.

Any student with one or more of these limitations, when confronted with a teacher using the Command Style, is an *a priori* deviant.

People who *will not* are those who have *made a decision* to resist. The only course of action open to them is to ignore and/or reject the command. Because of the rules of the style they cannot offer alternatives, and because of their constitutional or functional inability they cannot submit to the standard.

Regardless of why one becomes a deviant, a particular emotional state evolves from the fact of being different, unable, rejected. Under the Command Style there is no place for overt expressions of these emotional responses. People who are different and cannot adhere to the standards become *stigmatized*. The stigmatized person has no choice but to reject even more, and the chain of deviant behavior thus becomes never-ending. (For a thorough discussion of this process, see Goffman's book *Stigma* (23), which deals with both the stigmatized and the stigmatizers.)

Under the Command Style the treatment of deviants is usually *insistence* on required performance. The result is usually repetition of either the student's complete failure to perform or the teacher's rejection of another inadequate performance, and the vicious cycle goes on and on. When this kind of behavior becomes intolerable to the standard-setter (in this case, the teacher), the treatment is replaced by punishment designed *not* to rehabilitate the deviant but to save face for the teacher.

The Command Style and Systems of Reward and Reprimand

Punishment of deviants has two purposes:

1. To isolate or exclude the deviant;
2. To highlight the difference between discipline and deviant behavior by attaching to the deviant negative or lesser values—that is, denigration.

Examples of exclusion and isolation (used as reprimands) can be daily observed on the athletic fields and in the gyms of our schools. Although both places are presumably designed for the education of all students, in reality the Command Style (in its most perfect form in athletics) excludes many students from the very experiences that are supposed to aid them.

Isolation and denigration are prevalent in any reprimand system that is upheld and used by the Command Style of teaching. The grading system (by letter or number) is an illustration of the second component. In many cases the grade has nothing to do with what the student actually knows or has learned. It is a system designed to reward or reprimand those who are willing or unwilling to exhibit the behavior demanded by the Command Style.

These are gross examples. Equally powerful are all those daily personal moments when teachers exhibit acceptance or rejection of performance by word, deed, or gesture. All these cumulative experiences count in the way a child feels about what happens to him under the Command Style—the constant pressure to be good, to be better, to be as good as . . . , and so on.

Just as the reprimand procedures are compatible with the structure of the Command Style, so is the reward system. Approval is signified (by many techniques, in our schools) when a student has responded as designated, performed to the accepted level and form, *and* is willing to participate in the reward system. This last phase is important because it is often used by teachers as bait, motivation, and reinforcement.

The literature on the application of pressure to children is rich, and it is imperative that the teacher become acquainted with writings in it (23, 33, 36, 39, 46) to enhance understanding of the reward and reprimand rule as used in the Command and other styles of teaching.

Command Style and Verbal Behavior

The role of the teacher's verbal behavior in the Command Style has two main functions:

1. To initiate and create the aura and social-emotional climate conducive to this style.
2. To maintain this climate and sustain all the implications previously discussed.

To do this, a teacher uses primarily a declarative mode of speaking, which will include chiefly two areas of reference: (a) the structure of subject matter, and (b) the student's behavior.

a. *In reference to the structure of subject matter:*
    1. Stating that given facts are true or untrue.
    2. Describing events.
    3. Establishing boundaries of knowledge.
    4. Proclaiming values, truths.
    5. Assessing events (social, scientific, artistic, etc.)
    6. Others.

The teacher will also ask questions: particular *kinds* of questions designed to elicit only the content, values, and truth previously pronounced by the teacher, invoking primarily one cognitive operation: memory. At times questions will be aimed at another cognitive operation—understanding, but understanding the materials only according to the teacher's explanation.

Special phrases have become a part of a permanent teacher's vocabulary in this style: "This is the way to do it"; "The right answer is . . ."; "You are wrong, the right answer is . . ."; "The following are the three good things about . . ."; "I don't like what you are saying"; "You can do better than that . . ."; "Good boy!"; "Sit up straight!"; "Try harder!"; "Is that the way I told you to do it?"

This kind of language is intended to emphasize:

1. The teacher's value system.
2. Polarities (good/bad; right/wrong; slow/fast).
3. A student's placement on the teacher's hierarchy.

These three seem to correspond to the three sets of decisions in the Anatomy of the Command Style: pre-impact, impact, post-impact. Language reflecting the teacher's value system appears to support and maintain the pre-impact decisions made by the teacher. Language asserting polarities keeps tension up by reference to the speed, quantity, quality, and correctness of response which are part of the impact set. Language indicating the student's placement serves as a constant reminder that the teacher is the one who makes evaluation decisions, the post-impact set.

b. *In reference to the student's behavior:*
   1. Stating general rules of correct conduct.
   2. Announcing special rules for particular situations.
   3. Proclaiming boundaries.

Most (if not all) of the phrases used to convey these proclamations start with negative words: "No . . . ."; "Do not . . . ."; "You can't . . . ." These proclamations are often seen in school halls, gyms, and playgrounds in the form of a big poster that says:

One big *no* is the prohibition and next to it a list of all the anticipated violations.

The Command Style and the Developmental Channels

To proceed further in the discussion of relationships between the Command Style and the learner it becomes necessary to make some assumptions, if not give established facts, about what happens to the learner in this style. One way is to project the effects of the style onto the physical, social, emotional, and intellectual developmental channels, those dimensions to which the theoretical limits concept applies. It is assumed that man develops along these four dimensions (and perhaps others), and that these are interdependent, affecting each other in a reciprocal, complex manner.

For recording relationships between the style and each developmental channel, a schematic table provides visual clarity:

Theoretical Limits Concept

The Spectrum

Command Style	?	?				

Minimum ←   → Maximum
Physical development_____
Social development_____
Emotional development_____
Intellectual development_____

If an X were to be placed so as to best represent the effect of the Command Style on each channel of development, where would the X appear on each channel? Closer to minimum? Toward maximum? In the middle? Where? We need a criterion. Suppose we used as criterion the concept of the independent individual who makes decisions about himself and his destiny; then it is quite clear that under the Command Style the X will be placed close to minimum in all four channels.

1. Since all decisions are made by the teacher, the student can make no decisions about his own physical development.
2. Social development means interaction with others; prohibition of such behavior inhibits growth in this dimension.
3. A person who has learned to respond to commands by others (theoretically, in all areas) is emotionally dependent; certainly he lacks the opportunity for emotional growth that accompanies the emergence of an independent self.

4. Since all decisions are made by the teacher, and decisions require cognitive activity, the opportunity for growth along the intellectual channel is curtailed.

There are, of course, other criteria for evaluating the effects of teaching styles on various developmental aspects. These criteria might include dependent behavior, interdependent behavior, and so on. The reader might want to examine the placement of the X on the various channels according to various criteria.

4

The Shift in Decision Making: the Task Style

The Command Style in its theoretical form is a behavioral model at one end of a possible polarity. What would be a style of teaching akin to it yet different? — slightly yet *significantly* different? — a style that, indeed, can be designated as the second style on a continuum?

A logical way to solve this problem would be to design a theoretical model identical to the Command Style in all variables *except one*. So, theoretically, any style of teaching will suffice in which all decisions are made by the teacher and only one decision (other than the previously discussed decision to say *no*) is made by the student.

However, since any teaching style is both theory and practice, the second style will have to be described in terms of the particular forms of both teacher and student behavior that are the substance of the teaching-learning transaction. And since any possible teaching style will have all the elements of the Anatomy of a Style, the Anatomy must be examined to see where it will most logically yield a change from the Command Style that will produce the second style.

Of the three decision-making sets in the Anatomy, the *impact* set is the most logical, allowing us to make a *significant but minimal* change from the Command Style. To allow the first change to be made in the *pre-impact* or *post-impact* sets would produce too much change, because in the *pre-impact* it would allow the student to make decisions about subject matter, and even about the choice of style itself (and might, in fact, result in a behavioral model the *opposite* of the Command Style). We can make a meaningful change without yet going that far. And in the *post-impact* set it would, again, allow the student to make decisions, this time evaluative ones, about subject matter and style. So, only in the impact set will we find decisions that can be made by the student with no larger implications for the style itself or for subject matter.

Schematically, it looks like this:

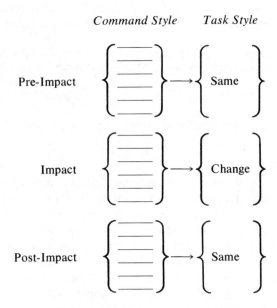

Command Style   Task Style

Pre-Impact ⟶ Same

Impact ⟶ Change

Post-Impact ⟶ Same

This change, this shift in *who* makes the decision in the impact set renders the following anatomy of the second style, we shall call the Task Style.

Anatomy of the Task Style

Pre-Impact Set
Who makes what decisions

Decision categories	Teacher	Student
All decisions	Makes all the decisions, as in Command Style.	Not involved.

Impact Set
Who makes what decisions

Decision categories	Teacher	Student
Whom to teach	Decides whom to focus greatest attention on, and how much.	Accepts the teacher's decisions.

What to teach	Makes *all* subject-matter decisions, as in Command Style.	Accepts the teacher's decisions.
Where to teach	Makes the *general* geography decisions, such as the location of a lesson, a laboratory experience, etc. Does *not* make *specific* geography decisions.	Accepts the teacher's decisions.
	Accepts decisions made by the student.	Makes *specific* geography decisions for himself, such as where to work or sit in the classroom, gym, cafeteria, assembly hall, etc.
	Does *not* make specific posture decisions; accepts those made by the student.	Makes *specific* decisions about personal posture for the activity performed: whether to stand, sit, kneel, relax, or whatever in order to facilitate his *performance* of the task.
Time decisions	Makes *general* decisions about occurrence—the beginning and the end—of the entire experience (since such decisions affect decisions about subject matter). Accepts all other time decisions made by the student.	Makes time decisions about the performance of the task with specific time components. These include: 1. Starting time of any single task within the given subject matter. 2. Stopping time of any single task— whether complete or incomplete. A decision to complete a task will satisfy the quantitative or qualitative decisions, or both. In this style, a *non-completion* decision is deviant behavior,

Anatomy of the Task Style (continued)

		because it curtails the teacher's subject-matter decision. 3. Interval, pace, and rhythm decisions.
Quantity decisions	Makes the general decision about "how much" or "how many," and specific quantity decisions as they pertain to individual students.	Accepts the decision and produces the required quantity — of pages read, for example, or straddle jumps made, or essay pages written.
Quality decisions	Teacher executes *all* quality decisions made in the pre-impact set (of major importance to proper execution of subject matter decisions), setting standards of performance for all aspects.	Accepts the standards.
Choice of teaching style	Follows the decision made in the pre-impact set.	Accepts.
Class climate	Follows the decision made in the pre-impact set.	Accepts.
Adjustment decisions	Teacher makes these as necessary (within the integrity of the style).	Accepts.

Post-Impact
Who makes what decisions

	Teacher	*Student*
Categories of evaluation decisions	Makes decisions about the kind, depth, frequency of evaluation, and about the *use* of the available evaluative information. *Comment:* It is the first	Not involved. Accepts evaluations made by the teacher.

time that the teacher *has
the time* to make evaluative
comments to *individual*
students without stopping
or interrupting the process
of communication with the
entire class.

Experiments with this style have shown that even during short periods, while students are executing single or multiple tasks, the teacher has the opportunity to communicate individually. This is a legitimate use of time for it is *not* at the expense of other students. In the Command Style, for a teacher to deliver individual evaluations during class would require interrupting the entire class and would flaw execution of the Command Style.

Availability of time provides the teacher the opportunity for *immediate feedback* to individual students. Furthermore — and perhaps of utmost importance — this immediate delivery of feedback (which may have positive or negative connotation to the individual student) is done in *private,* between the teacher and the individual student, while in the Command Style the student's privacy is constantly violated. Whether addressed to the entire class or to one student, comments are usually made publicly (the common rationale being that "you can't stop the flow of the lesson for one student"); every student knows to whom any comment is addressed. (Note that in the Command Style to stop the class and communicate with a single student, whether loudly or quietly, requires a parallel decision on how to prevent the rest of the class from meanwhile making their own decisions.)

To change from the Command to the Task Style, to these seemingly "insignificant" decisions from teacher to student usually creates a new class climate, a new feeling of self by both students and teacher, a new kind of relationship.

Many years' use of the Task Style of teaching in public school classes at all levels, in college, and in special programs (for example, a camp for brain-damaged, emotionally disturbed, or physically handicapped children) has shown the merits of the freeing process performed in *gradations* and has focussed on the need for *deliberate* attempts by the teacher to create experiences for the student in learning to make decisions.

The Process of Shifting Decisions

Let's talk about some of the hazards and problems implicit in the process of changing from the Command to the Task Style. How will such a change affect the behavior of students? What are some of the things a teacher should do to *facilitate* the shift, or should avoid doing so as not to *inhibit* the shift?

A student or class accustomed to the Command Style has attained a state of equilibrium; the students know what is *expected of them* and, in general terms, what to *expect from the teacher*. The very design of the Command Style dictates a particular kind of contract; the kind and level of expectation is clear and understood by both sides involved; the sets of stimuli and their responses are known. This, for good or ill, creates a sense of comfort: no unexpected moves, no surprises.

Any change in this equilibrium (no matter how noble the intent) creates some discomfort, suspicion, or hesitation. (The unknown usually does this to people.) Hence a shift in teaching style, which in effect is a change in behavioral expectations, will bring about disequilibrium, suspicion, and discomfort. Such a change is particularly threatening if it is abrupt, without previous notice or preparation and *clarification* of the new conditions, the new social and emotional contract. When a teacher's expectations change, most students do not know how to handle it.

Conversely, when students produce the expected new behavior, the teacher generally does not know how to cope with it. Neither student nor teacher is to be condemned: both respond as threatened people. (It must be kept in mind that here we are discussing *both* teacher and student accustomed *only* to the Command Style.)

Students will resort to retaliatory behavior, such as:

1. To ignore the new set of conditions; to not play the new game.
2. To pretend they do not understand the new conditions and expectations.
3. To sabotage the new attempt by the teacher.
4. To vocalize the failure of the new experience.
5. To mock the new behavior.
6. To openly reject the new conditions and resent the teacher for imposing them.
7. To abuse the new conditions by not learning.

These techniques are used by students regardless of age, level of achievement, or emotional stability. The only difference is in degree.

When teachers observe the disruption of their classes they generally respond in kind. They too retaliate, in such ways as:

1. First and foremost, to immediately (again demonstrating abrupt be-
    havior) *retreat* to the previous style, in this case the Command Style,
    to restore order and equilibrium and the sets of known mutual expec-
    tations. Teachers are familiar with the previous style, feel that their
    position in the transaction is not threatened in that style, and that re-
    lationship between sets of stimuli and responses can again be con-
    trolled. Students are familiar with the previous style and know that
    if noncompliance persists, the teacher's next step will be to invoke
    the system of reward and reprimand until equilibrium is restored.
2. To blame the students for not understanding or cooperating.
3. To blame the style of teaching for not delivering what its theoretical
    structure promised. (I have personally received letters and phone
    calls from distressed teachers who denounced this and other styles
    after an abrupt shift and only a brief encounter with its consequences.)

Fundamentally, this conflict occurs because the change is too abrupt.
One remedy is to make the shift in decision making gradual, even to the
point that the students in the class "exercise" the process—one decision
at a time. It is imperative to do the following:

1. To present a clear statement of expectation.
2. To state the new system of reward and reprimand.
3. To persist in the new style without retreat to the previous style in *any*
    of the decisions.

A clear statement of expectation helps the student know what the
teacher has in mind, providing him with the information needed to decide whether or not the new relationship is acceptable; it contains stipu-
lations about the teacher's new behavior, information needed before
the student can comfortably function in the new style. This information
is needed because students, particularly younger ones, *fear* unknown
responses by teachers. The clarity and consistency of the previously
known style help relieve this fear.

Because new roles for teacher and student rewaken this fear, it is
of prime importance to *announce* the new set of rewards and reprimands
and *act* upon it. Shifting some decisions to students means that today
they will *not* be reprimanded for doing something they were not allowed
to do yesterday. Moreover, yesterday's forbidden decisions are what
they are *requested* to make today. That the same response is reprimanded
one day and rewarded the next is disturbing and creates behavioral chaos.
(We have seen classes accustomed to the Command Style in which students literally did not know *how* to make geography decisions, time decisions, and so on—presumably "small" decisions, but they could not
make them. They were so conditioned to certain sets of S-R behavior
that they could not demonstrate the shift—certainly not an *instantaneous*
shift.)

It is quite obvious that time is required for this process, as for any process — perhaps more so when it comes to behavioral changes. Teachers will find that they must repeat explanations of the new expectations; students will make a few tests to find out if the teacher "really means it," and will seek out reinforcement for their new behavior more frequently than before.

The results of this process are rather rewarding to both teacher and student. Primarily it is an emotional reward, because it represents the beginning of *mutual trust*. At this stage of the evolutionary process trust is a new dimension for both teacher and student. It should be quite clear from its structure of decisions that the Command Style is *based* on lack of mutual trust: the need for the teacher's proximity and rigorous control and surveillance project this lack of trust. The Task Style elicits and rewards the beginning of trusting behavior. *The introduction of trust reduces pressure, which in turn reduces the use of retaliation.* This new reality affects both teacher and student; a new climate is developing a new feeling of self. It is a tiny step but a *critical* one, because it is a first attempt at alternatives to the Command Style, an attempt that opens up *further* possibilities of development. It is critical primarily for teachers and students who are philosophically or emotionally committed to the Command Style.

During many seminars and demonstrations of this process to many teachers across the country, we have seen teachers fail to perceive the shift in decisions that students were accomplishing before their eyes. It seemed as if their philosophical commitment to the Command Style kept whispering, "It is not right; students can't make decisions." In addition, they could not see themselves in the suggested new role which requires them to relinquish decisions, a position which is emotionally incongruent with their previous state of balance and security. Overcoming this barrier takes time to learn how to shift to the new style, to experiment with the operation of the style, and for the teacher to examine his own reactions and adjustment behavior.

Operation of the Task Style

The next problem is the daily practice of this style. Three issues need to be considered before implementation:

1. Alternative decisions about organization.
2. Alternative views of subject matter.
3. Alternative communication techniques.

1. Alternative Decisions about Organization

The two major components to be reorganized are geography and time, since the decisions the student makes about these components must be to use space and time in ways different from those of the previous style.

The four organizational formats possible are:

a. Single station/single task
b. Single station/multiple tasks
c. Multiple stations/single task
d. Multiple stations/multiple tasks

A. Single station/single task   Here the class remains one unit in which everyone is engaged in the same task. Some examples are:

The entire class is seated, each student in his respective seat (the student can decide on the location of the chair, etc.), and the entire class is engaged in one task, for example, spelling a particular word. Time decisions, starting, pace, etc., are made by students.

In a physics lab, each student is at his place and everyone is engaged in the same task — say, observing the parallax phenomenon.

In music class, each student with the instrument of his choice, in his own location, all learning to produce the note C.

In the gymnasium, all in the "regular" class formation, engaged in a single task: 10 sit-ups.

Examples can be cited in all subjects. This arrangement is valuable when only *one* task is being taught as an introduction to an activity or experience, because members of the class are enabled to make some impact-set decisions without disrupting the customary organization of the class.

The shift can be introduced to young children decision by decision as a game, which they enjoy a great deal. They are proud to exhibit their collective ability to make one, two, three, . . . , seven decisions in the performance of one task, any task. Needless to say, when a class exhibits this behavior the teacher needs to acknowledge and reinforce it: "I see that you can do it," "I am pleased with the way you did it," etc.

The single station/single task arrangement is very helpful for teachers whose fear of losing control makes them hesitant about using the Task Style. This arrangement, only a small step from the Command Style, can be comfortable for teachers experimenting with the shift.

B. Single station/multiple tasks   In this arrangement the class is still one organizational unit but the students are asked to engage in *more* than one task — their number to be decided by the teacher because this is a subject-matter decision. If one wants to be a pedant, one can proceed systematically in "shaping the behavior" of the class by introducing two, then three, four, five tasks. Some classes may need this kind of ordering, while others might be able to move from one or two tasks to clusters of several. Examples of clusters of tasks in various subjects are:

In spelling:

   i. Writing the particular word once
  ii. Writing a second word
 iii. Signaling to the teacher readiness for individual checking of the spelling

In the physics lab:

   i. Observing the parallax phenomenon
  ii. Shifting the position of the pins in relation to the glass
 iii. Observing the new condition
 iv. Checking for parallax

In music:

   i. Sounding the note C once
  ii. Sounding the note D once
 iii. Sounding the note E once

In physical education:

   i. 10 sit-ups, curled trunk
  ii. 10 sit-ups, straight trunk
 iii. 10 sit-ups, straight trunk, bent knees

C. Multiple stations/single task In this arrangement the class is divided into smaller groups that disperse into different station-areas in the class, gymnasium, auditorium, etc. Each station has a task designation to be preformed by each student.

Can you think of examples to illustrate this arrangement?

D. Multiple stations/multiple tasks In this arrangement the organization is the same as in the previous one, but the students engage in several tasks at each station.

Can you think of examples to illustrate this arrangement?

During performance of the task(s), in any of the four organizational formats, the teacher's role provides for:

a. Moving about the class
b. Observing individuals without disturbing the rest of the class
c. Evaluating individual performances
d. Offering feedback to individuals

Thus the availability of time to be involved in decisions of the post-impact set is perhaps the most important asset of this style in terms of teacher's contribution to the class.

When this style is in full bloom these organizational alternatives bring about new perceptions of time and space, and the actual *use* of time and space becomes more efficient. Spaces in classrooms, gymnasiums, and labs that previously were unused — even unnoticed — become populated, and previously congested areas become less so. Time is used more efficiently: more students individually perform tasks most of the available time, because the feeling of self-control and self-direction in decision making is developed. The use of time has become more relevant to the individual student. It is possible to reach the point at which a given class will become self-starting and self-sustaining at the cluster of tasks, within the boundaries of subject matter known to the class.

2. Alternative Views of Subject Matter

Subject matter   Development of a theoretical framework for teaching behavior cannot ignore subject matter and the relationships that exist, actually or potentially, between a teaching style and subject matter. We must clarify the concept of subject matter — or even more so, the concept of the *structure* of subject matter. "Subject matter" and the "structure of subject matter" are two different concepts, two different kinds of pedagogical idea.

Subject matter traditionally means *a body of information* (usually an aggregate of facts in a given investigative area) that is delivered one way or another to the students. This can be seen in many school curricula, as curricular guides, booklets for courses of study, handbooks, and textbooks.

These subject-matter materials usually contain a collection of facts arranged in chapters, units, etc., in order to accommodate the teacher or the school calendar, and are often either the product of an author's idiosyncracies or a committee's compromises. They are the work of a selective process that often thwarts the student's interest, denies opportunites to expand knowledge, and at times even circumvents the truth. Many of these materials appear as *final statements*. This, of course, is a violation of intellectual integrity, because there are very few pieces of knowledge that are final statements or the only "truth."

The structure of subject matter   The *structure* of subject matter deals with *a body of knowledge,* as opposed to a body of information; it contains related facts, postulates, principles, theories integrated into generalizations, comprehensive models, perhaps universal truth. A body of *information* is limited, fragmentary, restricted to practical or operational needs. A body of knowledge is limitless, coherent, flexible, and universal. In mathematics, details of the use of the slide-rule are information; the mathematical concept behind the slide-rule is knowledge. Individual grammatical rules are information; the concept relating them to the structure of communication in a given language is knowledge. The words and notes of a specific song are information; the relationship of these notes to a musical scale, musical phrasing, and style is knowledge. Changing spark plugs or tires or pumping gas deal with information; understanding the operation of the engine and the relationships among its components is knowledge. A particular exercise on the parallel bars is information; understanding the relationship between man and the parallel bars, kinesiologically, physiologically, is knowledge. Examples like these can be observed in every area of the curriculum; probably every such area is composed of *a body of information* and *a body of knowledge.*

Now, if it is true that the characteristics of information call for use of the Command and Task styles, and perhaps others, then the characteristics of knowledge call for use of entirely different styles of teaching. One of the major *differences* between these two clusters of styles is which *cognitive operations* each requires, and how much. Styles conveying information mainly utilize *connecting* (as presented by the teacher). Obviously, dealing with a body of knowledge requires styles of teaching that elicit and develop many more cognitive operations. These processes are given fuller analysis in the styles that appear later on the spectrum.

Task Analysis

In the Task Style of teaching, although it is theoretically permissible to present the student with any single task or multiple tasks, operational efficiency calls for an additional consideration: which *kind* and *sequence* of tasks will provide the student with the opportunity to accomplish the objective of the lesson in minimal time, effort, space, etc. This requires *task analysis:* the dissection of an event into its components, which may produce a few "large" components or many "tiny" ones. This too depends on the teacher's decision about the usefulness of the size and number of tasks in accomplishing the objectives of the lesson.

Task analysis, which must not be confused with analysis of the structure of subject matter, is for immediate purposes within a particular context. Analysis of the structure of subject matter is for long-range, conceptual purposes, independent of particular circumstances. For example, an analysis of the event called "walking from the classroom to the auditorium" where several sub-tasks are observed, such as lining up in twos, walking through the halls, keeping to the right of the traffic, entering the left auditorium door, etc., is an example of a task analysis. A kinesiological analysis, involving both anatomy and physics, of the act of walking represents analysis of the structure of subject matter.

To aid in the selection and distribution of tasks in the Task Style the following guides are offered:

1. Time sequence analysis
2. Movement sequence analysis
3. Space (geography) sequence analysis
4. Special rules of the event-sequence analysis

1. Time sequence   Every event takes time; the components of the event are always arranged in a chronological sequence: things that occur first, second, . . . last. So a task analysis of any event can use time as the sequence criterion. Time sequence can be:

Intrinsic   An example is any biological phenomenon that is species specific: for example, all humans must *first* develop enough strength in the legs and the trunk *before* they can walk. Intrinsic time sequence means the sequence *must* occur at all times and under all conditions.

Artificial, or agreed upon   This will include all the time-sequenced events conceived, designed, and implemented by man. This is usually done for convenience or efficiency, as perceived by the decision maker. Practically every *procedure* in school exemplifies this. (Also, there are excellent examples in industry, the armed forces, etc.) In fact, the very word "procedure" projects the intent: "This is how to proceed," which means using a particular time sequence.

2. Movement sequence   Every physical human act involves movement (can you think of an exception?), which involves sequence. Particular events involve particular sequences of movement. For example, the act of writing involves: finding a writing implement, picking it up, carrying it to the writing surface, moving it in particular ways, a particular sequence to form linguistic symbols, etc. Any experiment in chemistry, any event in the library, in music, in shop, in mathematics involves a sequence of movements. Categorically movement sequence involves all the decisions about "how to do it."

Can you suggest the sequence of movement instances that occur (or might occur) in events of your subject?

3. Space sequence   Clearly, space sequence is integral with time and movement sequences, since any event occurs in some place or places. So, space and location can help determine the sequence of tasks. (A cafeteria is an example of this kind of sequence. Certain tasks are done at a certain time in a certain place: tray and tableware are taken, food is selected then paid for, a table is found, the food is eaten.) The integration of decisions about these three sequences is epitomized in the assembly line.

4. Special rules of the event-sequence analysis   Sometimes, the decisions about tasks that affect all three sequences are bound by the "rules of the event." Examples of this are a school assembly, a wedding reception in a particular subculture, or a diplomatic reception. The sequence of tasks in these events is set by predetermined rules, derived from either social manners, or the need for crowd protection, or respect for tradition.

Now, regardless of the criteria for selection, a task analysis can make the teacher more aware of what is to be done and what is being done in the class. While this awareness is developing, the teacher who is engaged with the students will also become more aware of how these task-sequences affect the feelings of the students. There is always the question, "What did a given decision do to, for, or against the student?"

Are there other sequence analyses that might be made in order to select and distribute tasks in the Task Style of teaching?

3. Alternative Communication Techniques

The delivery of tasks to be performed requires some insight into communication possibilities. The discussion above implies that alternative techniques in communication are needed, techniques fitted to the teaching-learning transaction of a particular style. The model on the next page is for classroom communication, on the assumption that since the classroom is *not* a *micro*cosm, but rather a *part* of the *macro*cosm, some events in life do not ordinarily occur in the classroom, and therefore, some communication techniques are not used in the classroom, certainly not deliberately.

Let's first examine the model's components and their interrelationships, then its use in the spectrum of teaching styles and the effect that

Classroom Communication Model

1 Content	2 Mode	3 Action	4 Medium	5 Direction	6 Time
Information Knowledge Feelings Other	Audio — output / input	Speaking (other sound systems) / Hearing	The teacher Tape recorder Record player Telephone Other	T → S T ← S T ↔ S S ↔ S T ↔ T	Min. ↔ Max. Duration Frequency Immediacy
Information Knowledge Feelings Other	Visual — output / input	Showing / Seeing	Teacher's performance model Teacher's gestures Films TV Books Other	T → S T ← S T ↔ S S ↔ S T ↔ T	Min. ↔ Max.
Information Knowledge Feelings Other	Tactile — output / input	Touching / Being touched	By teacher (directly) Via mediators (other people or things) Other	T → S T ← S T ↔ S S ↔ S T ↔ T	Min. ↔ Max.

each style has on the choice of a *communication set*. As the model suggests, there are six components to a given communication set:

1. Content
2. Mode
3. Action
4. Medium
5. Direction
6. Time

All six *must* exist for communication to occur. The interrelationships among these six components are the *communication set*.

Content   Communication always conveys *something* from one person to another; an idea, a question, a feeling, a mood. All these are content: you cannot communicate *nothing*. In this model, the kinds of content are: information, knowledge, feelings, etc.

Mode   Man is intrinsically capable of several modes of communication. We use all or some of them with different degrees of frequency and skill, but they are always poised for use when there is content to communicate. This classroom model presents three modes of communication:

1. Verbal
2. Visual
3. Tactile

Action   Each mode of communication has its own action: the verbal mode always involves *speaking,* output, and *hearing,* input. Unless one person *speaks and* another *hears,* there has been no verbal communication between them. The tactile mode involves *touching* and being *touched,* whether to communicate feelings, rules, controls, and so on. So the content to be delivered depends on the use of a mode of communication, the mode depends on the action.

Medium   Any action in any mode can be conveyed only by a *medium,* not without one. The verbal mode with the action "speaking" uses the following *media:*

1. The teacher   Voice and language are used to communicate content. (Eloquence, clarity of phrasing, control of voice help the teacher become a more perfect medium.)
2. Tape recorder
3. Record player

4. Telephone
5. Television (a two-mode medium)
6. Films (a two-mode medium)

The *visual mode* by the action "showing" uses the following media:

1. The teacher
   a. Showing a model of performance (demonstrating)
   b. Using gestures
2. The student
   a. Showing a model of performance
   b. Using gestures
3. Books
4. Charts, diagrams, maps, three-dimensional models, etc.
5. Slides
6. Pictures
7. Film or film strip
8. TV

The *tactile mode* by the action "touching" uses the following media:

1. The teacher (direct contact)
2. Others besides the teacher (indirect contact)
3. Objects (indirect contact)

So, content depends on mode, which depends on action conveyed by a medium.

Direction   There are several possible directions for the *flow* of communication:

1. Teacher to student
2. Student to teacher
3. Both ways
4. Student to student
5. Teacher to teacher

These four apply to the verbal, visual, and tactile modes and to *all* media (except in the category of "student to teacher" when the teacher is the medium and "teacher to student" when the student is the medium).

Time   All communication takes time: teaching a whole course, or a fleeting wink—both take time. Time has three aspects in communication:

1. Duration. Answering the question, "How long to communicate?"
2. Frequency. Answering the question, "How often?"
3. Immediacy. Answering the question, "How soon?"

All three are on a minimum-to-maximum continuum. The *duration* of communication can be minimal (theoretically and operationally it means zero time or no communication) or maximal (theoretically, infinity of time), or in-between. The frequency can be minimal or maximal (theoretically, minimum: never; maximum: all the time. It is determined by the size of the interval).

Immediacy refers to the time-lapse between output and input, which, of course, depends on the medium. A book is an example of temporally *remote* communication. (For example, do you know when this book was written?) "Live" television is an example of *instant* communication.

Operation of the Model

As previously stated, a given communication set is composed of six components: content, mode, action, medium, direction, time. Let's follow the dialectics of each set.

The Verbal Communication Set

A decision to communicate a given content is followed by a choice of three modes. Say the verbal mode is selected. Next the medium must be chosen for the action "speaking," since every medium has advantages and disadvantages despite the fact that they convey the *same* content:

$$\text{content } X \begin{cases} \text{a speaking teacher} \\ \text{a "speaking" tape recorder} \\ \text{a "speaking" record player} \\ \text{others} \end{cases}$$

The *message* is the message, rather than "the medium is the message." That is not to deprecate the importance or power of media, which can hardly be disputed, but merely to comment on the use of media in the schools — often under the guise of curricular innovation when there has been no innovation at all. The same content is still presented, but in perhaps a more efficient way — a problem made more acute by the claim that new media have renovated teaching. The exaggeration of such a claim is particularly obvious in relation to television. Television is, however spectacular, merely a recording device. The lens and the microphone record what is to be seen and heard. If a teacher behaves by the Command Style, television will record and convey the Command Style. The *teaching* has not changed, only the *medium* bringing the Command Style to the student has changed. In the same way, books or charts are conveyers of teaching, but do not themselves teach because media cannot make decisions, they can only convey them.

Back to the process of the verbal communication set. Once the medium is selected, the direction of flow is decided. Is the medium to serve the teacher only? the student only? both? Obviously, the answers depend upon the style of teaching. For example, in the Command and Task styles, media will be used mainly for conveying the commands, the decisions made by the teacher, as in a TV lecture or demonstration conducted by the teacher on the screen: the direction is from teacher to student. If, on the other hand, other styles that call for student decisions are used, media must be made to allow communication to flow from student to teacher.

As the direction decision is executed, time decisions must be made. How often and how long does the teacher speak? How often and how long does the student speak?

These decisions can be schematized by circling the choice in each component of the communication set and connecting them by an arrow.

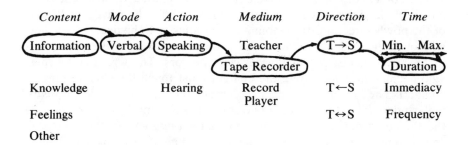

This could exemplify the Task Style in teaching folk dancing, reading the constitution in a social studies class or a poem in an English class, or any other activity appropriate to any other subject.

The Visual Communication Set

The process and sequence of decisions are similar to those in the verbal set. After the content decision is followed by a decision to use the visual mode a rather wide choice of media confronts the teacher.

Selection requires scrutiny of a wide variety of possibilities. What is the best way to *show* the content? A demonstration? Who will demonstrate? Is the teacher skillful enough to demonstrate flawlessly? Maybe an expert on film is more desirable? A certain content may be available only in one medium, say a film about a particular expedition.

Sometimes combined media will have a greater impact—for example, the dissection of a frog with color slides of different stages of the dissection. Should a book be used? Which one? How can the school's TV equipment be used? What kind of a picture display will present the desired point of view (particularly important in, say, sessions on current events)? How can a display present different points of view? Who selects the pictures for display?

Suppose a decision is made to have two-way directions in communication (T ↔ S). Does the teacher accept all the pictures brought by students for display? Does the teacher exclude some? Which ones? Why? Do the decisions made in this set fit the style of teaching?

What if the content is "feelings"? How does the teacher use himself to show feelings—joy, elation, satisfaction, displeasure, anger?

The Tactile Communication Set

In some pedagogical areas the tactile set of communication is possible, in others desirable, in some essential. At times, a violin teacher will physically lead the bow hand of the student to offer the player the "feel" of the bow's direction. In tumbling, gymnastics, and the like, the teacher will touch the student in order to assist the performance of the movement or to guard against potentially hazardous errors. The wrestling teacher who decides to demonstrate the content must touch the student (direct contact). The life-saving teacher to demonstrate must touch the "drowning" student (direct contact). If two students serve for the demonstration, the tactile communication is by a mediator (indirect; another person). In teaching fencing, the tactile communication also occurs by a mediator, an object: the foil or the saber (wink, Sara).

An angry teacher might communicate the intensity of his anger by grabbing a student's arm. Conversely, a teacher might lovingly but firmly restrain an angry child whose expressions of anger might cause damage.

Causes of Failure to Communicate

The more aware a teacher becomes of the intricacies of communication and their implications to the emotional climate of the individual and group, the more effectively can he select the appropriate style of teaching.

This model for classroom communication not only helps one understand the function of communication, it can also alert teachers to causes of communication malfunction. If the stimulus does not elicit the expected response, the communication has malfunctioned. Sometimes the cause can be found by retracing the sequence of the communication-set and checking it against the original intent; every decision must have been appropriate to the chosen style of teaching.

If we keep in mind that a child does not perform a task because he either cannot or will not, then, while retracing the communication-set, consideration must be given to the following possible reasons for the breakdown:

Physiological reasons   Some children do not hear well, others do not see well; some have limitations of their perceptual input, integrative, and output mechanisms. Any one or combinations of these curtail, and, if extreme, eliminate, the quantity and quality of participation in the communication process.

Emotional reasons   There are legitimate emotional reasons which limit or prevent a child from participating in any mode of the communication process. Some of them are: anger, embarrassment, distrust, fear, unhappiness. Of these genuine emotions, any one may cause a breakdown in communication. We have all experienced them: it is *all right* to experience them. Teachers must learn to acknowledge them: first acknowledge the feeling, then treat it. Never abuse it!

Cultural reasons   There are legitimate cultural inhibitors of participation in the communication process. Cultural inhibitions are a result of inability to "read the clues" or understand the symbols—such as language and gestures—used in any of the modes of the communication set. Inability to understand the symbols may cause anger, embarrassment, distrust, fear, unhappiness, any of which may stop the communication.

These cultural symbols reflect values. Any failure to understand and respond to one of these reduces the efficacy and flow of communication. Inability to understand most or all *stops* communication. Such breakdowns are quite familiar to students who come from foreign cultures or from various American minority subcultures.

Personal reasons   There are legitimate personal inhibitors of communication—primarily interest. There is genuine interest and genuine uninterest. Uninterest prevents communication.

Let's plot the relationship between the Task Style and the developmental channels. Where would you place the X on each developmental channel to represent the Task Style?

Theoretical Limits Concept

Command Style	Task Style	?	?	?
Minimum←				→Maximum

Physical development_____
Emotional development_____
Social development_____
Intellectual development_____

5

The Reciprocal Style

At this point the visual model for the decision shift from the Command to the Task Style looks like this:

	Command Style		Task Style
Pre-Impact	{ }	same →	{ }
Impact	{ }	change →	{ }
Post-Impact	{ }	same →	{ }

The decision shift from teacher to student has occurred in the impact set and only in decisions concerning geography, time and posture (starting, stopping, duration, pace). All other decisions remain part of the teacher's role.

The question now is: Where is the *next* shift? Let's examine the possibilities. If the student were to make decisions in the pre-impact set, the entire content of the transaction (including subject-matter decisions) would be a result of student's decisions. This would be too big a jump at this point. Later styles on the spectrum will handle this condition. Now we seek to provide a teaching-learning transaction akin to the Task

Style, yet different—a transaction that will occupy the next position on the theoretical spectrum and will also serve as an operational possibility in this evolution. This leaves us with the decision shift in the post-impact set.

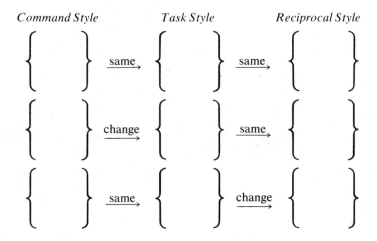

Command Style   *Task Style*   *Reciprocal Style*

The third style, which we will call the Reciprocal Style, is evolved by having students making post-impact decisions that evaluate their execution of tasks in the impact set.

Now, since the teacher cannot really evaluate every student all the time in a transaction with more than one student nor can the teacher be available for it, it becomes feasible to adjust the class organization to accommodate the one-to-one ratio and provide for students' decision making in the post-impact set.

This organizational adjustment calls for working with a partner—not a partner in a random array of roles but one who is *actively and specifically* engaged in decision making. (Other roles for the partner, such as holding an instrument in the chemistry lab, turning the page in music, spotting in physical education, listening to a reader in English, although important and relevant to the experience, are only helping roles in the Reciprocal Style.)

So, the class is divided into pairs, composed of two actively participating partners: one the *doer,* the other the *teacher,* whom we will call the *teacher-partner* to avoid confusion with the class teacher. Including the teacher of the class we have an interacting triumvirate of three carefully defined roles.

Teachers are often concerned about reorganizations of their classes to offer greater possibilities for interaction and communication among students. (See the classroom communication model, Chapter 4.) This concern (and at times fear of loss of control) raises the question how to divide the class into pairs without disturbing the equilibrium that has existed under the climate of the previous styles.

There are several procedural (and logical) possibilities:

1. The teacher assigns the partners.
2. The teacher and the class discuss the possibilities and *agree* on a selected procedure.
3. The students themselves pick their partners.
4. Others?

The first procedure prevents the student from deciding with whom he wishes to share the experience. In fact, it will contradict the very process that this style is designed to promote, that of *socialization*. Essential to learning to socialize is the opportunity to decide with whom to socialize. (We'll handle the fear of presumed "discipline" disruption below.)

The second procedure sounds good but has its own hazards. Since the Reciprocal Style is the first on the spectrum that provides for active socialization, some students may not yet know how to go about it and may therefore refuse to try it, while others may prefer to abide by the teacher's selection. This may occur for several reasons:

a. The student does not trust himself (memories of previous unsuccessful attempts to work with others).
b. The student does not trust others (same reason as a.).
c. The student does not know what to do.
d. The student wishes to follow the teacher's choice.
e. The student thinks that the teacher wishes to make this choice—and tries to flatter the teacher by accepting the imposed choice.
f. Others?

It does not matter which actually causes the inhibition; the important point is that any of these might block the first step in socialization: the mutual choice of partners.

The third procedure not only shifts to the students an additional and vital decision, it conveys that the teacher has *trust* in the student.

In the reality of the classroom, the fact is that most, if not all, children and older students can select their own partners. Those who cannot select or are not selected need help; additional time is needed to find out the causes and remedy. (Being and working with others is not being promoted here as a *virtue:* it is recognized that it is proper to be alone at times.)

How do students tend to select partners? There are two main ways:

1. They *mutually* select their equal.
2. They *mutually* select their nonequal.

Equality can be viewed from either the teacher's or the students' point of view. Clearly, to be consistent with this style of teaching and with the process of shifting decisions, the students' view of equality must be honored. Their measuring devices, which often differ from those used by teachers, are more accurate and relevant to their emotional state when they select partners. (No sociograms can beat the spontaneous expression of need to associate with somebody *now*. By the time the data are assembled and tabulated, the sociogram is outdated. Children shift their social choices, sometimes fast and frequently; the Reciprocal Style accommodates this reality.)

Equality in the selection of a partner-to-be depends upon two sets of criteria:

Functional criteria   Equality or inequality of height and weight, as required for the performance of a given gym activity; equal skill and knowledge in performing a chemical experiment or playing a duet; equal verbal skills in preparing for a debate; the sameness or difference in sex, as needed for performance of a task.

Emotional criteria   Physical attributes are not the determining factor, nor skillfullness of performance; rather, *emotional affinity* motivates the social proximity: "We like each other, we want to be partners," is the statement underlying the choice. Now, in the Reciprocal Style, who chooses the selection criteria? Of course, there is always the possibility of integrating both the functional and emotional sets of criteria.

One aspect of the student's view of equality might concern some teachers. Students who select their equals usually do so because they see themselves as "good" or they know the teacher feels they are "good kids." But sometimes students choose each other because they see themselves as equally "bad kids." This expectation is perhaps the source of the teacher's concern and fear. Indeed, both situations require further observation by the teacher, further gathering of information about what constitutes "good" and "bad" kids in the classroom. Is it not possible that the teacher's fear is premature? Two students who are "bad" separately may not necessarily combine to one "bad" pair. Is it not possible that the teacher's notion of "good" or "bad" is questionable? Is it not possible that their realization of the new trust in them might diminish their "badness"? Students who like each other and want to be together might overcome the need for individual deviation and join in successful and appropriate participation. It's worth the attempt.

What about students who select the unequal partner? Why would a successful student select the failing one? Why would a weak student latch on to the strong?

These analyses and questions can heighten the sensitivity of teachers to a variety of psychological interpretations and insights involved in the presumably insignificant act of dividing a class into operating pairs. It is important to consider these possibilities during the shift to the Reciprocal Style. This process of reciprocation intrinsically demands a variety of adjustments by all three members of the triumvirate.

The next step is to identify the roles of the teacher-partner and the doer. (The teacher-partner and the doer switch roles once a task or a series of tasks has been terminated.) The doer, who is engaged in execution decisions and performance of the tasks delivered by the class teacher, is actually engaged in decisions of the impact set. It is the teacher-partner who learns to make post-impact decisions. In order to make some of the post-impact decisions, the teacher-partner must engage in several operations, perhaps sequentially:

1. Knowing the task(s).
2. Knowing the performance criteria (quantitative, qualitative, or both).
3. Observing (seeing and/or hearing).
4. Comparing and contrasting.
5. Concluding.
6. Communicating with the doer.

1. Knowing the task(s)   Both teacher-partner and doer receive the task description and delineation from the class teacher, by the communication set, decided by the teacher. (More details will be presented below, in the discussion of the teacher in the Reciprocal Style.) It is imperative that the teacher-partner understand the task and all its details.

2. Knowing the performance criteria   Both teacher-partner and doer must know the details of the quantity and quality of the task(s) to minimize the chance of misunderstanding or disagreement between them about the criteria. Such prior equality of understanding will minimize the potential emotional tension caused by the process of being evaluated by a peer.

Because the teacher-partner must understand the criteria in order to compare and contrast *before* judging the performance, understanding is the only condition that can lead to a genuine delivery of results to the doer.

3. Observing   (What a marvelous opportunity to learn how to look, how to see.) This is the first active step in the teacher-partner–doer relationship: the teacher-partner observes the doer attentively and perceptively, in order to gather information — of a very special kind: information about his peer, what he did, said, thought, or felt. Because this information will be presented back to the doer, to do it as accurately and as genuinely as possible the teacher-partner must learn to observe, to see. (Sometimes it is helpful to practice this act of seeing: a task can be presented; a volunteer performs it, and each member of the class offers his observation, which is then checked against the criteria.)

4. Comparing and contrasting   "Compare and contrast" is inevitable. Whenever criteria are derived from an experience, it is extremely common to compare and contrast subsequent similar experiences to it with those criteria: "This car is bigger than . . . ," "This woman is more beautiful than . . . ," "This idea is as . . . as . . ." When we look at things or people, listen to sounds, feel textures — our perceptual mechanisms select and organize the information into categories. This organizing and categorizing is made possible by the process of comparing and contrasting, a cognitive operation in which man is engaged a great deal of the time.

The Reciprocal Style of teaching provides for this operation in a deliberate way. The more one deliberately compares and contrasts, the more one learns to perceive.

5. Concluding   Drawing conclusions *always* follows the operation of comparing and contrasting; one cannot avoid conclusions, they are intrinsic to the process. Even if you conclude that there is *no conclusion,* a conclusion has been reached. So, steps four and five form one cognitive flow.

6. Communicating results   Since in this style there is a one-to-one ratio between performer and evaluator, it has the advantage of immediate feedback and knowledge of results. Once the teacher-partner has observed, compared the information against criteria, and drawn conclusions, conclusions can be delivered to the doer by itemizing the observation in the sequence given by the criteria's details. Children of all school ages seem able to do this.

After this communication the task is either terminated if successfully performed or repeated if corrections or adjustments are needed. This decision is made by the class teacher and conveyed to the teacher-partner and the doer via the criteria details. If the criteria are quantitative, the task is finished once the required quantity has been reached; if the criteria are qualitative, the task is done once it has been performed sufficiently well. Both kinds of criteria can readily be recognized and followed by the teacher-partner. Once the task or tasks are done, the two students switch doer and teacher-partner roles, the tasks and the cycle of impact and post-impact decisions begin again. The *reciprocal* process has begun.

The Teacher's Role

So far we have discussed the reciprocal roles of teacher-partner and doer: teacher-partner ⟵⟶ doer.

What is the teacher's role in this three-way relationship? What things must the teacher do or not do in order to avoid a reverting to previous styles?

Let's start with what the teacher must not do. The three-way relationship can be schematized:

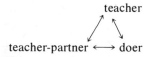

This seems to be reciprocal in all directions and to fully involve all three participants. The purpose of this style is to develop a *particular* relationship between teacher-partner and doer, a particular process, particular abilities, a particular emotional climate of mutual trust and comfort. Therefore, it is important to restrict and delimit the behavior of the class teacher.

Because the teacher has shifted post-impact decision to the teacher-partner the teacher *does not communicate* with the doer during the post-impact time, but only with the teacher-partner:

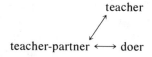

The class teacher is not meant to be remote, but only to restrict his role so that the two student partners can enhance *their* ability in decision making. A teacher who communicated with a doer would have usurped the teacher-partner's role and destroyed the very process this style seeks to develop. Many teachers will at first find it difficult to maintain a restricted role. It is easy to imagine a teacher notice that a doer is incorrectly executing a task and intervene spontaneously, presenting observations directly to the doer, and thus violating trust in the teacher-partner. Teachers in all areas show this inability to refrain from immediate corrective statements.

From this kind of teacher behavior the student draws several conclusions:

1. The teacher does not trust me.
2. The teacher told me that I can and should make decisions, but isn't patient enough to allow me to learn how.
3. I cannot really believe what the teacher tells me.
4. I do not have the opportunity to develop this exciting and responsible new relationship with my partner.

Such realizations by students bring about an emotional climate that must be resolved. Rarely can a student tell the teacher about these violations. More often, both student partners retreat from the Reciprocal Style, cease to perform their reciprocal roles, and the entire process stops.

For these reasons, the class teacher must communicate only with the teacher-partner, and in a way that projects the teacher's sensitivity to the new position and role of the teacher-partner. This can be accomplished either by acknowledging the teacher-partner's performance of evaluation ("I see that you have learned to observe the performance," or "You know now how to use the criteria for evaluation purposes,") or by asking questions that elicit confirming information ("Do you need to know anything else in order to talk to the doer?" "Do you see something about the doer's work that is different from what you have on your criteria list?"). Asking questions of this sort will help redirect the teacher-partner to focus on the criteria and the process of comparing and contrasting. The teacher-partner will thus be made to feel less threatened and more comfortable about the process. The class teacher must not moralize or criticize the teacher-partner for the doer's failure to perform. If the comments are not helpful, again, the process will cease, the teacher-partner will refuse to participate in this three-way relationship.

(*Comment:* Teachers who are hung up on subject matter and the administrative concept of "covering materials" may need more time to learn to use this style. Experience has shown that once this process is in motion, *more* "materials" can be covered in *less* time. It is all a matter of trust. What an opportunity for the young to learn that they can be a part of adult decision-making, and for adults to learn what the young can really do.)

Once this style has been internalized by the class, one can observe their weaning from previous styles. It is fascinating to observe students genuinely engage in all the post-impact decisions.

While the Reciprocal Style is in process, several *hazards* may appear.

The nature of the transaction requires these to be anticipated—even expected.

The potential hazards of this style of teaching include:

1. Physical hazards
2. Emotional hazards
3. Social hazards
4. Perhaps some intellectual hazards.

1. Physical hazards   In subjects such as physical education, shop, or home economics, where physical activities predominate, or are a good part of the task, it is possible that the teacher-partner may not be able to detect a potentially hazardous deviation from the task. This potential hazard requires an additional awareness by the class teacher and a more detailed presentation of the task(s) with special emphasis on the safety problems. (We teach safety awareness not by avoiding the task but by understanding and diagnosing the problems and by practicing the safety procedures.) When danger is *imminent,* the class teacher intervenes and stops the action; the problem needs to be re-explained, the task demonstrated again, details reviewed, and the process continued.

2. Emotional hazards   When two students work together and are involved in reciprocal evaluation, there are many potentials for emotional tension.

Evaluation by a peer is laden with possibilities for insults, harassment, degrading comments, and negative implications. Conveyed by word or gesture, these may trigger embarrassment, anger, and covert or overt retaliatory behavior. Teachers using this style with young children need to be alert to these possibilities. It has been observed that in most cases of reciprocal evaluation, students with both positive and negative observations present to their peers *negative* statements *first!* One can imagine what feeling such a presentation creates in the doer: discomfort and failure.

Why do children do this? Because they have usually heard negative comments and criticism first from their teachers? Because such teacher behavior has left so deep an impression on the young that when they are called upon to make an evaluation they imitate what they have internalized?

What do you do when you are engaged in post-impact decisions? Which information do you deliver first to your students—the negative or the positive? Do you tell them first about their failures or their successes? How are you reacting to these questions right now? Do you feel that these questions hint to *your* successes? failures?

It takes time for a child to learn to accept the peer and the performance of the task and to learn to deliver the evaluative information with
minimum or no threat. Children can learn to use phrases such as: "You
have performed the task five times as prescribed. I think you need more
time to work on . . ." instead of: "You stink! You can't even do . . ."
The differences in connotation and emotional climate are clear.

The class teacher must learn to be alert and sensitive to the sounds,
words, phrases, and gestures used by the students so that abuses, insults, negative treatment can be detected as soon as possible.

Sometimes a child delivers false information to his partner, either by
overpraising or underpraising him. This is particularly possible in tasks
that *require* an outside observer because the doer cannot sufficiently
observe himself while performing.

When any of these hazards occur, the class teacher must do something to relieve the emotional tension. Two approaches seem to work
well: if many teacher-partners are behaving in any way that creates one
or more of these hazards, it may be appropriate to have a discussion
with the entire class about how to talk to one another or how to exchange
information without abuse; if instances of abusive behavior are infre-
quent a private talk with the pair or the teacher-partner alone may be
sufficient.

In a TV program conducted by the author to demonstrate the
Reciprocal Style, after a task involving a physical activity had been
performed by a group of doers, their peers, the observers and evaluators
stood completely silent. When the group was asked why the silence,
there was no response. Finally a girl (9 years old) was asked directly:
"Why aren't you talking to your partner?" She replied: "I don't want
to hurt his feelings."

"Why would you hurt his feelings?"

"Because I have bad things to tell him."

"Do you have any good things to tell him?"

"Yes!"

"Then, why did you not tell him the good things?"

She hesitated and then said: "I don't know."

A group discussion followed immediately, on the air, about the different ways of delivering information, and the consequences of each
way. It was decided to *experiment* with saying good things first, the task
was repeated, and positive communication began first.

3. Social hazards   These are directly connected to emotional
hazards. The essence of the Reciprocal Style is a specific kind of socialization. Because the social contract is clearly defined, any emotional
hazard can overpower the need for social association and possibly end
the relationship between the partners. Mutual accusations and retreat
from the social contract are prevalent in this style. In order to enhance

the social unit, the pair, and its mutual activity, emotional tensions need to be handled without the destruction of the unit.

4. Intellectual hazards When this style has been presented to thousands of teachers across the United States and Canada, one of their most frequent questions is, "What happens when the student gives wrong information?" Or they respond to this style with, "Children cannot teach each other; they don't know enough." It is true that this style presents a potential though slight intellectual hazard, but any error in information can be corrected later. Errors occur, but teachers themselves make errors. Careful task presentation and criteria delineation will reduce this potential hazard. Then again, one of the purposes of this style is to enable the student to learn the importance of accuracy in transmitting information.

There are several ways of transmitting information, especially criteria, from the class teacher to the teacher-partner:

1. Oral presentation, with a demonstration if necessary.
2. Task cards. Index cards of any size on which essential data are recorded by the teacher. The major components of each task are recorded on the card, and the performance criteria as well. The more accurate the description of the task and the performance criteria, the greater the potential for accurate observation and evaluation by the student.
3. Mimeographed sheets
4. Wall charts
5. Three-dimensional models
6. Slides, film strips, etc.
7. Others?

All these are technical aids *only,* designed to record the teacher's decisions and make them available to the student at any time, so the student can remain aware of the objectives of the tasks, task analysis, behavioral objectives, and so on. With young children we call these aids "things to look for," with older students "task details," "criteria," etc. (The language should always accommodate the linguistic level of the learners.)

The Reciprocal Style and the use of different media for information and performance-criteria advance the individualization process a step further.

**Use of the Group in the
Reciprocal Style**

A variation of this style is to use more than two students as the reciprocal unit. The anatomy of the style remains the same, but the organization and distribution of functions and the social-emotional conditions are different.

The unit is enlarged to three, four, possibly more participants; each additional one becomes a teacher-partner and has a *particular* function in the relationship with the doer. There can only be as many members as there are specific interacting evaluative functions in the relationship with the doer: for example, recording, judging, correcting, timing, etc. By systematic rotation each member fills the different available roles.

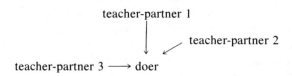

Some tasks require simultaneously observing quantity and quality and recording results. While the doer performs the task, teacher-partner 1 can observe and assess its quantitative aspects (by judging against criteria), teacher-partner 2 observes quality, and teacher-partner 3 records the results uttered by the other two. When the doer completes the task the three teacher-partners convey their information to him: the doer is the *focus* of the organically operating group and each teacher-partner is *directly connected* to him by some role. For complicated and detailed tasks that require more than one observer and evaluator, each teacher-partner can observe a specific part of the task.

Physical education provides excellent examples. Some physical tasks are complex. No one person can observe all the details of the performance; too many movements occur in a short period of time, say in certain stunts in tumbling or gymnastics. One teacher-partner can observe the movements of the head, another the movements of the trunk, a third the exact position of the toes, and so on. Obviously, the feedback here will be minute and probably more accurate than if there were only one teacher-partner.

Can you suggest examples in your field where it is possible (and perhaps even feasible) to develop a group reciprocal process? Can you dissect some tasks to provide for this organic relationship?

This arrangement is workable, for many tasks, in terms of task execution, motivation to continue, immediate feedback, and so on. Nevertheless, adjustment decisions in the interwoven social and emotional domains seem inevitable. The hazards in the relation between one doer to one teacher-partner are multiplied by every additional teacher-partner, as is the likelihood of retaliation. Imagine the doer feeling besieged by "vultures": it is difficult enough to learn to listen to the critical statements of one peer—how much more so when confronting several? A high level of tolerance seems necessary if a group is to operate reciprocally over a period of time.

Because it is as difficult to learn to convey evaluative information as it is to learn to receive it, permanent efficacy of the group depends on its members' emotional controls, linguistic sensitivity and social affinity.

On the other hand, a successfully operating group, skillful in information exchange and emotionally stable, must fill its members with a special feeling of pride and esprit de corps, of mutual accomplishment, a sense of group purpose and support, and the feeling of power that attainment brings.

It should be clear by now that group involvement in the Reciprocal Style is fundamentally different from procedures called group discussion, T groups, encounter groups, group sensitivity training, and the like. In the Reciprocal Style one person performs a specifically defined task and is temporarily observed by several others who seek specific observations, deliver specific judgments based on specific criteria, and offer specific closure that terminates the experience. (Perhaps the reader with experience of any of these groups and procedures could try to place such an experience on the spectrum as it evolves.)

Implications of the Reciprocal Style

The Theoretical Limits Concept

First, let's observe our position on the developmental channels.

Theoretical Limits Concept

Command Style	Task Style	Reciprocal Style	?	?	?

Minimum ←   → Maximum

Physical development_____ ?	
Emotional development_____ ?	
Social development_____ X	
Intellectual development_____ ?	

It is obvious that the Reciprocal Style has moved the X on the social development channel much closer to the maximum pole. This is because most decisions about social interaction (choice, observation, and evaluation of the partner, and delivering immediate information) are made by the student.

Would you care to replace the question marks on the other developmental channels with properly located Xs?

Deviant Behavior

A major form of deviant behavior in this style would be *not* to communicate with the partner — quite a reversal from the Command Style. This style is designed for interaction, for exchange, for *talking* to each other, for socializing. Any student who does not engage in these behaviors, whether it is because he cannot or will not, is exhibiting deviant behavior in *this* style.

This contrast in evaluation of *identical behavior* from one style to another illustrates one of the most powerful aspects of the spectrum: *dialectic relativism.* Dialectic relativism enables us to focus on the changeableness of the relationships in the teaching-learning transaction, a changeableness intrinsic to the structure of the spectrum, for *each style occupies a position in the decision-making continuum.*

Dialectic relativism is important in understanding deviant behavior, since, logically, behavior can be deviant only if there is a standard. And a standard reflects *a* philosophy of education. The spectrum of teaching styles presents self-sufficient but coherently interconnected alternative behavioral models in a structure that can reflect an array of philosophical stances. The spectrum is not eclectic, it is cohesive, integrated.

Systems of Reward and Reprimand

In the Reciprocal Style, communication, learning to observe and to assess performance against criteria, and talking to a partner and conveying appropriate information are rewarded. Teachers who were taught by the Command Style and are now teaching by it find it difficult to reward such behaviors. To do so seems in conflict with what they consider right and wrong classroom behavior. It is important for these teachers to realize that such rewards are congruent with the structure of the Reciprocal Style. The issue is *not* Reciprocal versus Command, but that the Reciprocal Style has its *own* systems of reward and reprimand different from those of another style. The theoretical design of one style cannot be viewed by the *value system* of any other style.

Similarly, behavior will be reprimanded in the Reciprocal Style only when it is deviant in terms this style. Again, a teacher who is a novice in this style will find it difficult to reprimand *only* behavior which is incongruent with *this* style. We can see that "discipline" can no longer be thought to have only one definition, nor can it be defined according to a teacher's personal point of view.

Implications for Philosophy
of Education

The Reciprocal Style represents a philosophy that places a degree of trust in the student and in his ability to make those decisions congruent with this style. Shifting post-impact decisions to students significantly changes the roles and responsibilities of both teacher and students. Teachers who do not subscribe to this philosophy, although they can understand this style, *cannot behave* according to it, because their belief that they have relinquished responsibility and some control will prevent them from making the theory operational.

Implications for Organizational
Procedures

This style necessitates considerable adjustments in classroom organizational procedures:

The very beginning of the lesson might be different. In this style, students enter the class and proceed in pairs to their respective areas of work and begin their tasks. It is possible, of course, to assemble the class as in the Command Style for general administrative announcements, roll call, etc., but this kind of behavior by the teacher puts the class, momentarily, in the Command Style. Though it is permissible to do so and then continue in the Reciprocal Style, surely these things can be done in ways congruent with the Reciprocal Style. How would *you* check attendance or communicate administrative details in the Reciprocal Style?

Distribution and collection of equipment and materials will be different. This is quite relevant to laboratory sessions in chemistry, physics, and biology. Since the students can make time and geography decisions, equipment and materials can no longer be distributed by the teacher according to his decisions about time, place, sequence of distribution, etc., for this would be a violation of trust. Having the students do so in their own pace, speed, and sequence will constitute enhancement of trust. Can you see the relevance of these comments to other subjects? All? (Any exception? Why?)

Classroom traffic will be different. There might be constant mobility in the class, but purposeful mobility related to learning. This, again, requires adjustment by the teacher. Many classes in many subjects in many schools are still conducted with high degree of *immobility*. In many places, sitting still is considered a virtue. Moving about to get or exchange equipment, to read instruments, to accommodate space needs, to be alone with a partner, and so on are correct in the Reciprocal Style; independent, purposeful mobility is necessary for its operation.

Other classroom organizational procedures?

Implications for Verbal Behavior

Who talks to whom   To reiterate, the structure of this style calls for two communicating units: teacher-partner and doer; class teacher and teacher-partner. These are the operating units during the actual process of reciprocation. During delivery of the task(s) and performance-criteria, the teacher communicates with the entire class; schematically:

Task and criteria delivery:
$$\text{class teacher} \searrow\searrow\downarrow\swarrow\swarrow \text{all teacher-partners and doers}$$

Reciprocation process:
$$\text{class teacher} \nearrow \text{teacher-partner} \leftrightarrow \text{doer}$$

In both situations the students may communicate with the class teacher or teacher-partner by asking questions for information or clarification of the tasks.

What is said   The content of the communication between the teacher and the entire class includes: the tasks, their details, quantitative and qualitative statements related to them, a demonstration of techniques, citing of sources, etc. The content of the communication between the class teacher and the teacher-partner includes: delivery of performance criteria, periodical observation by the class teacher of the evaluation performance by the teacher-partner, asking questions for information and clarification, making suggestions to the teacher-partner about the evaluation process, and offering him feedback about his performance as an evaluator. The content of the communication between the class teacher and the doer includes: the initial delivery of tasks simultaneously to all doers, and periodic observation, of the doer's performance only.

At times, the class teacher must observe the doer, to gather information that will help him communicate with the teacher-partner. By observing the performance of all the doers the teacher informs himself about how successfully the class is performing.

The content of the communication between the teacher-partner and the doer includes: observation of the doer's performance; feedback to the doer, which includes statements of acknowledgement (for example, "I see that you can do that.") information concerning the performance, corrections, requests for repeat performance, and reinforcement. The doer can communicate with the teacher-partner by asking for information and clarification.

When reciprocation is first begun, the doer will often seek to communicate with the class teacher, from whom all the students are accustomed to seek approval.

This attempt to communicate will be a delicate moment; the teacher can hardly say, "You are not supposed to talk to me, this style does not provide for this." There are good reasons for the doer to seek contact with the teacher: it had been customary and pleasant, and had made the student feel important during contact, and had produced information, etc. It is difficult to suddenly have to seek all these from a peer.

Such a moment will perhaps be most delicate with young children, who may feel rejected by an abrupt refusal from the teacher. There are various ways of handling it; one way is to walk with the doer to the teacher-partner while saying, "Let's go over to your teacher-partner and find out what we need to do." "Your partner has everything you need to know written down." "Remember, today your partner is your special teacher." In this way, and in other ways that are possible, the child's obvious need has not been sacrificed to the "purity" of the teaching style.

How it is said   Special attention must be continually paid to communication between teacher-partner and doer. Words have not only meanings, but also connotations: the power to trigger feelings. It is vitally important that students be made aware of this so that some of the emotional hazards previously discussed can be avoided, especially since any evaluation is criticism, which has its own impact on emotions.

**Implications for
Learning**

Since the individualizing process which began in the Task Style is continuing, and the students are making more decisions about themselves in the context of specific tasks, learning seems to be enhanced on two levels: quantitative and qualitative.

When students learn to be on their own and make decisions in matters of place, time, pace, etc., they stop being dependent on stimuli from teachers — often stimuli that were paced and sequenced inappropriately for many students. Learning to be one's own decision maker in these aspects enables one to learn more in general.

Qualitatively, the Command and Task styles adhere to the S-R (stimulus-response) learning models whereby the student's role is mostly responding. But the physiology and psychology of responding are limited, because responding by S-R means lack of choice, lack of time to hesitate or make judgments, and therefore minimum employment of the myriad cognitive operations available. The Reciprocal Style, although it is a continuation of the Task Style in the impact set for the doer's behavior (which is within the S-R model), provides for the beginning of additional cognitive behaviors by the teacher partner. Since the two partners change roles during the transaction, all students in the class can benefit from this new dimension, a part-time involvement in some cognitive operations. (The role of cognition in teaching behavior will be more thoroughly discussed later in our study of the spectrum.) The chief cognitive operations now involved are comparing, contrasting, and drawing conclusions, all done by the teaching-partner; this three-step operation calls for cognitive involvement other than a stimulus-response. Comparing and contrasting means deciding the value of things, seeing and understanding the parts and perhaps the whole of the things compared, and reaching a conclusion by weighing information against criteria.

And it matters not how "important" the issue: to compare and contrast the shape, color, and function of a pencil with those of a book of matches (which is a lovely comparing-and-contrasting game) involves the same process as to compare and contrast the American, Egyptian, and Chinese revolutions. The content is different; the cognitive process is the same. The Reciprocal Style provides for the deliberate beginning of these operations.

Schematically the Reciprocal Style in operation might look like this, in relation to positions of the Xs on the developmental channels.

Theoretical Limits Concept

Command	Talk	Reciprocal	?	?	?

Minimum ←   → Maximum

Physical development			X	
Emotional development		X		
Social development				X
Intellectual development	X			

6

The Individual Program (Teacher's Design)

Let's shift decisions again, the next is still in the post-impact set, from teacher-partner to doer himself. In this style, because the doer is engaged in self-evaluation, he is making decisions in two sets: the impact and the post-impact, schematically:

	Command		*Task*		*Reciprocal*		*Individual*
Pre-Impact	{ }	same →	{ }	same →	{ }	same →	{ }
Impact	{ }	change →	{ }	same →	{ }	same →	{ }
Post-Impact	{ }	same →	{ }	change →	{ }	change →	{ }

Decisions in the pre-impact set, primarily those about subject matter, are still the teacher's. The student's decisions in both the impact and post-impact sets adhere to the content decisions of the teacher.

The main aspect of the Individual Program is that the student, presented with the entire program, chooses that task and the level of performance within it that he considers best suited to him at the time.

The Anatomy of the Individual Program (Teacher's Design)

Pre-Impact set
Who makes what decisions

Decision categories	Teacher	Student
1. Content decisions	a. Selection of the general area to be studied and the specific subjects and topics. b. Specific tasks are selected and arranged either at random or in sequence. (This depends on the structure of the lesson (usually called the lesson plan) and the structure of the subject matter.)	Not involved.
2. Criteria decisions	Quantitative, qualitative, or both. These must be designed and stated clearly in a way that will not interfere with the flow of students' execution of the tasks.	Not involved.
3. Geography	At this point on the spectrum, the teacher makes only general geography decisions, never specific ones.	Not involved.
4. Time	General time decisions. It is conceivable that the teacher will never make specific time decisions during the entire operation of the Individual Program; this may last one class period or several weeks.	Not involved.
5. Climate decisions	The teacher's decision here is only a subsidiary one. The climate and discipline that prevail are implicit in this style, are logically determined by selection of the style.	Not involved.
6. Communication decisions	The teacher decides about the communication-set to be used in the delivery of the program itself, the tasks and the performance-criteria.	Not involved.
7. Anticipated learning style	The decision is implicit in the kind of tasks included in the program design.	Not involved.

Impact set
Who makes what decisions

Decision categories	Teacher	Student
	The teacher's role during impact is primarily to make individual contact with each student, observing, and giving assistance and support to those who request it.	
1. Geography	Accepts student's decision as long as the general geography decision or student involvement in the session are not negated or restricted.	Selects the location of the performance. If movement from one area to another is required, the student decides about it.
2. Time	Accepts students' decisions: as long as general time decisions are not negated there is no conflict with intrinsic demands of the style.	The student makes *all* specific time decisions. a. *Starting* When to start the program in any given lesson, or a particular task, or a cluster of tasks. b. *Stopping and Interval* The length of each task; all decisions about stopping a task; the length of the interval between different tasks are made by the student.
3. Climate decisions	Selection of teaching style determines class climate; execution of the program in the impact set produces the class climate intrinsic to the style. The teacher's execution decisions about climate must remain consistent with the style even when individuals in the class demonstrate behavior inconsistent with the style. Deviation by a student must be handled individually.	The climate of a self-operating class requires not only highly disciplined behavior, but above all the student's *self-discipline.*
4. Communication decisions	The teacher responds to student communication in a manner consistent with the style.	Students decide about the use of the communication-set when they need to clarify any point in the program.

The Anatomy of the Individual Program (Teacher's Design)
(continued)

Post-Impact set
Who makes what decisions

Decision categories	Teacher	Student
	Teacher gives students feedback (corrective or reinforcing) regarding the teacher's observations of the student: 1. his ability to meet subject-matter demands 2. his operational level of self-direction as prescribed by style 3. his involvement with self-evaluation 4. others Indeed, this style provides maximum opportunity to focus on individuals during all three phases of the teaching-learning transaction. Comment: If intervention to make clarification is necessary, it is done with minimum interruption of the student's decision making.	Student evaluates his own ability in relation to subject matter demands made by the teacher.

There are a variety of designs or formats of Individual Programs, all individualized on different levels and requiring different kinds of responsibilities and responses from different individuals. All Individual Programs present several tasks and a range of performance for each task, and have several important dimensions in common:

1. All objectives to be accomplished are specific and defined.
2. The tasks require and develop a high degree of independent performance.
3. They require and develop the ability to function independently for prolonged periods of time—an important factor. A successful performer of an Individual Program has learned to free himself from dependency on immediate stimuli from the teacher and has become capable of prolonged self-responsibility by carrying out a program of multiple tasks.
4. They serve as a continuous motivation for improvement.
5. They make progress highly visible, by allowing both student and teacher to view at a glance the progress of learning and performance

by looking at the markings on the individual program designating the student's present status.

6. They are an excellent diagnostic tool for differentiating performance levels in a heterogeneous class. (Some teachers will think it desirable to maintain instant control by spot checking the performance of individuals; but this technique, though it might seem useful in large classes, violates the sense of trust that has been developed.)

7. They provide for recognition and acceptance of individuals as they are.

8. They free the teacher from the requirement that he constantly emit stimuli.

9. They provide the time for individualized contact with students.

This style is represented by several operational designs:

Design 1: Programmed learning (or programmed instruction)
Design 2: The quantitative individual program
Design 3: The qualitative individual program
Design 4: The combined individual program (multiple levels of performance differentiation).

The format for all designs includes general information: name, grade, number of the program, subject matter, etc. This may seem superfluous, but if over the year a teacher needs to prepare many of these programs the bookkeeping and storage become a problem that can be reduced by the vital information at the top of the program.

The paragraph "to the student," containing pertinent information on program and performance requirements, is important because:

a. It informs the student about the logistics of the program.

b. The student can read the information individually, eliminating the need for class ceremonies.

c. The need for repetition of logistical details is eliminated. (*Only* the information pertaining to *that* specific program should be included, since it is intended to be a guide for action.)

Individual Program

Name of Student _____ Date Started _____
Grade _____ Subject _____

To the student:

1. The tasks below are organized in a program for you. Your role is to follow this program at your own pace. If you need any further information about the task feel free to consult your teacher.

2. At the completion of each task, check the appropriate column.

Task description	Criteria (performance details)	1	Levels 2	3
1.	a.			
	b.			
2.	c.			
	a.			
3.	b.			
4.				
5.				
6.				

Student's questions or comments: _____

_____

_____

The task description includes the general assignment designation, for example: Read Chapter 7; Answer questions 1–25; Do experiment 7; Practice the hook shot; Play part one of the concerto. It sets the subject-matter boundaries for the given program. In the criteria section are the *specific details* on performance of the given task, the behavioral objectives relevant to it, which, of course, involve task analysis, distribution, and sequence, and subject matter and the structure of subject matter.

It is particularly important to realize that the Individual Program (teacher's design) teaching style is found in schools, under such names as individual work sheets, contract, and others. However, what counts is not the fact that the student makes some decisions, but rather what *kind* of decisions they are. When projected against the anatomy of a style, most of such individual programs are revealed to be variations of the Task Style.

Many kinds of "programmed learning" materials fall into this category. Since the literature on programmed learning or programmed instruction is vast and available, there is no need to analyze operational Design 1 in this book. (However, for analysis and design purposes, or just for the fun of it, project such a program against the anatomy of a style and observe the results.)

Quantity and Quality

Before we can examine the next three operational designs, quantitative, qualitative, and combined, it is absolutely necessary to examine the concepts of *quantity* and *quality* in the assessment of human per-' formance and task design, because any decision made in the post-impact set of the Individual Program is based on a quantitative and qualitative assessment. In fact, any task design involves decisions about quantity and quality, does it not? (Can you think of any task, in any area, that does not *intrinsically* possess these two attributes?) Since our program designs are becoming more complex, we must clarify these attributes and their relationships to different kinds of tasks. Otherwise, programs will be developed and assigned that are at best *random* in the presentation of tasks, which is not intellectually honest because it subjects students to arrays of tasks nebulously connected and arbitrarily sequenced, yet presented as if they were the truth.

Value Systems

There are several ways of examining quantity and quality and their application to task analysis and program design: first, the three value systems that affect judgment about the classification and categorization of tasks:

the functional value system
the assigned value system
the intrinsic value system

The functional value system   guides decisions about inclusion or exclusion of tasks according to their usefulness. For example, to a coach a particular basketball shot (the particular movement-task that produces that shot) has utilitarian value: if the shot went into the basket, that movement task is good, has value (in fact, a prescribed and identifiable value – 2 points!). This movement-task would merit inclusion in the program, because it is functional.

To a music teacher a particular finger combination in a difficult passage of a violin concerto might have utilitarian value. Since that passage has to be played regardless of its difficulty, the finger arrangement that helps play the passage is included in the task selection: it is functional. (Can you suggest a functional task in mathematics, social studies, English literature?)

The assigned value system   guides decisions about choices and placement of tasks by personal judgment or group consensus. Both are culturally determined. The performance of a task in gymnastics is good or beautiful or neither in the personal judgment of the observer or observers. Its value is *assigned* by cultural standards. A musical performance, a painting, a reading of a poem, a political argument are subjected to the assigned value system which either accepts them as good (and, if applicable, valid) or rejects them as undesirable. This decision determines the fate of the task(s) and their placement in the program. Can you identify instances in your field where tasks are included in programs based on assigned values?

The intrinsic value system guides decisions about choices and placement of tasks based on attributes which are specific to the subject matter and inherent to its structure. They are true and universal, they cannot be affected or changed by personal or group opinion, pressure, or consensus. The gravitational law and all its formulae and related experimental tasks represent the intrinsic value system. Inclusion of tasks and sequences of tasks related to the subject matter depends on the understanding of its structure, not on the mood, personal choice, or preferences of the teacher.

The tasks involved in teaching the quadratic equation have a logic intrinsic to the subject matter itself not affected by personal opinion, political affiliation, or mood: relationships among the factors in a quadratic equation represent the intrinsic value system. Another example is selecting tasks for an individual program in teaching anatomy: the parts of an organism, their relationship to one another, the physical laws that govern the function of the organism are intrinsic to anatomy.

In designing an individual program, this distinction among the three value systems—which are not necessarily mutually exclusive—helps clarify the criteria for task selectivity and the criteria for performance evaluation. This clarification is necessary for the integrity of the post-impact decisions. For example, if you design an individual program in social studies to include a sequence of tasks (say, reading tasks followed by written question-and-answer tasks) that reflect a particular point of view, it is imperative to recognize that this particular program embodies the assigned value system: the evaluative interpretation of events stems from *a* point of view, which is *not* necessarily the "truth," the only possible evaluation of the events.

It is particularly important to recognize this distinction among value systems, because in the student's new reality—that he is making evaluative decisions about his own performance of tasks—he must know that a particular program represents *a* point of view rather than *the* point of view. In this style, an individual program of tasks following a lesson on the American Civil War cannot be presented in general terms glorifying the causes of freedom and condemning the forces of oppression. Specific tasks (except the facts of dates, places, etc.) in the individual program must possess statements of value judgments, beliefs, and so on. Because "The Civil War was fought to free the slaves" is an assumption often presented as fact, it must now be announced as such: "This individual program represents a particular value system, the teacher's or a particular historian's or philosopher's."

Such teaching behavior accomplishes several things. It conveys what is presently considered the truth, and, in so doing, informs the student about a particular point of view, and allows the student to *accept or reject* the interpretive parts of the individual program.

Such behavior also informs the student that his own evaluation of his performance (in the example above, his knowledge of the interpretation of certain events) is based on criteria derived from the declared value system. He has the choice of *knowing it* but not *accepting it*. This will probably apply to all individual programs incorporating the assigned value system. An example of the limitation of, and potential distortion resulting from, self-evaluation under the assigned value system is a program of tasks in human movement; in tumbling, some tasks are usually included in the program with specific performance "rights" and "wrongs," often reflecting the choice of the teacher, or a committee, or simply tradition, which *stratify* the tasks and performance and *stigmatize* those who cannot adhere to the specific, presumably, "right," performance details.

This reality, totally based on the assigned value system, is alien to the concept of the Individual Program, which is designed to accommodate individual differences when each student is making many decisions. To avoid distortion, this individual program in tumbling (and similar programs in other fields) must *declare* that its design and evaluative criteria are based on the assigned value system. Only then can the individual student know his position — relative to knowledge, or performance, etc.: relative *only* to *that* criteria.

Similar distortion, and consequent potential failure, often occur in English classes, particularly in the area of writing styles. When an individual program of tasks requires from the student written statements about ideas, events, feelings, and so on, unless the writing style is specified by the teacher (by the assigned value system, of course, a personal one in this case) the student will not be able to make appropriate post-impact decisions and evaluate his performance of the writing tasks, and the post-impact decisions will have to be made by the teacher — which is a retreat from this style of teaching.

The assigned value system seems to promise conflicts, confusions, and distortions *unless* it is clearly announced that a given program was designed under the guidance of the assigned value system, and the same is true of the functional value system, so that students can understand (and perhaps accept) the reasons for the given program. An extreme example is a program designed for safety in an emergency, when each person must perform so many tasks in time to escape the hazard. You do certain things, in a given sequence and amount of time because it is functional in saving your life. When a student practices his program and evaluates his performance, success is measured by functional criteria; how fast you can leave the room and jump through the emergency exit counts, not how good you looked doing it. The latter represents an assigned value, the former a functional one.

Some mathematical problems can be solved in many ways; each solution is good by the functional value system because it solved the problem. Yet, mathematicians talk about an "elegant solution." Is this a combination of the functional and assigned value systems?

This discussion on the three value systems that affect task selectivity is meant to alert the program designer to the different values that can inhere in a given task included in a program for individual learning. Some readers, particularly those who hold values to be the core of any educational discussion (this is not meant to deprecate this philosophical position) will claim that value systems should appear at the beginning of any education treatise. The three value systems have been discussed here because it is the first time on the spectrum that the student makes post-impact decisions about himself—decisions requiring a broader knowledge of the *reasons for* performance expectation levels, which always reflect a value system. Now, there is a very interesting relationship between the three value systems and the quantity and quality demanded in any task.

The *quantity* of a task is how much—in numbers, height, weight, length of time, speed, depth, etc. About such tasks as writing, reading, playing an instrument, running, jumping, etc., one can ask the following questions, here phrased in reference to reading:

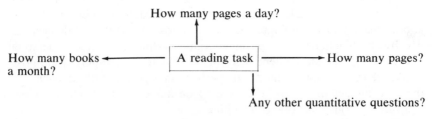

These quantitative *factors* are part of reading and, therefore, an individual program in reading can be designed for tasks in each of these factors:

Level 1 — read pp. 1–10 in a given book
Level 2 — read pp. 1–20 in the book
Level 3 — read pp. 1–25 in the book
Level 4 — read pp. 1–*n* in the book

— and so on. This array is bound by a quantitative measure of the task: the number of pages required to be read.

A time factor, also quantitative, can be introduced into the program, which now will look like this:

Level 1 — read pp. 1–10 1st day
Level 2 — read pp. 1–10 2nd day
Level 3 — read pp. 1–10 3rd day

and so on. *Two* quantitative factors now determine the task design. Obviously, it is possible to introduce a third factor: speed (more specific time boundaries). The program will look like this:

Level 1 — read pp. 1–10, 1st day, one hour to complete the task
Level 2 — read pp. 1–10, 2nd day, ¾ hour to complete the task

and so on. An individual program in reading can be based on one or any number of factors that determine the quantitative differentiation of tasks.

Let's take a writing task:

How many pages an hour? ← A Writing Task → How many words per minute?

How big is the handwriting?

How many pages on a given topic?

Other quantitative questions?

Again, these factors are part of writing and affect the tasks selected for a program. For example:

Level 1 – copy the following two pages once
Level 2 – copy the same two pages twice
Level 3 – copy the same two pages X times

As with the reading task above, any of the quantitative factors can be applied to a writing task – handwriting size, pages per hour, etc.

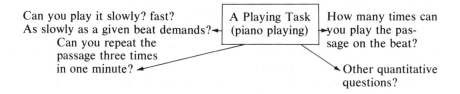

Here too the tasks are differentiated by quantitative factors which affect the assembly of tasks into a program. You cannot have a playing task on the piano without the factors of speed, rhythm, etc.

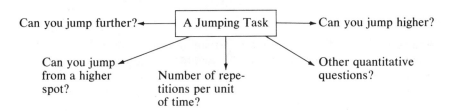

Again, height, distance, and perhaps other factors are part of any jump task. Since no jump is without height, distance, or both, a program of jumping tasks can be designed in which these and others are the differentiating factors.

Any task can be quantitatively distributed for a program by identifying its quantitative factors for use as measurable criteria for the design and performance of the program. Some more examples:

The task of hammering a nail depends on:

a. the size of the nailhead
b. the length of the nail
c. the thickness of the wood
d. the size of the hammer's surface
e. the weight of the hammer
f. anything else?

An individual program for the task of hammering a nail can be designed using an array of tasks *differentiated* by each of these factors. (This approach of quantity and quality differentiation in task analysis for the design of Individual Programs proved extremely helpful in working with neurologically impaired children. For further details see the forthcoming book by Mosston and Mueller: *Teaching Children Who Cannot.*)

The task of writing letters is affected by the following factors:

a. the size of the letters
b. the thickness of the letters resulting from
c. the thickness of the pen point
d. the slant of the letters
e. the density of the letters (closeness to each other)
f. the thickness of the pen body
g. the speed of writing
h. others?

The task of throwing a ball is affected by the following factors:

a. the size of the ball
b. the weight of the ball
c. the distance of the throw
d. the height of the throw
e. the speed of the throw
f. the direction of the throw
g. others?

Can you do this kind of "factor analysis" in various tasks in your field?

The *common* aspect of all these quantitative factors is that they are all *intrinsic* to the task. Hence they represent the intrinsic value system. Thus, we can reduce any task to its quantitative factors:

General Scheme for Task Differentiation: Quantity

Task description	Quantitative differentiation by:							
	Numbers	Weight	Height	Thick-ness	Speed	Depth	Dis-tance	Other
	From the smallest number to the largest applicable to the task.		From the smallest unit of the given factor to the largest applicable to the task.					

The quality dimension of a task answers the question, "How well?" How well is the task perceived, comprehended, and executed? Or, "How well do you see? How well do you perceive? How well do you relate bits of information? How well do you interpret? How well do you read? How well do you play ball?" Such quality questions, which can be asked about many tasks in many fields, must be answered if the student is to make post-impact evaluative decisions.

What are the criteria for answering quality questions, what are the *sources* of the answers? What does it mean when we say, "He writes well," "She paints beautifully," "He understands well"? The answers to these questions come from *sets of standards* established by individual or group judgments, in the form of rules, aesthetic standards, traditional sets of responses, etc. They are culturally determined and agreed upon and represent the *assigned value system*, the sole determiner of the qualitative dimension of task differentiation. Therefore, in the school *any* task to which the intrinsic or functional value systems do not apply invariably represents the assigned value system. Examples abound in any school: the school song, the dress code, gym uniforms, acceptable ways of addressing the teacher, a way of writing one's name and dates at the top of an assignment, certain procedures and behavior in the cafeteria, most procedures and behavior required in the assembly hall, certain classroom procedures used to assess how well students do. All these and many others are tasks determined and shaped by the assigned value system. Can you identify in your classes and in your field tasks which fall into this category? Who assigned the given values to these tasks? You? The principal? The Board of Education? The students? Unknown sources?

General Scheme for Task Differentiation: Quality

Task description	Qualitative differentiation by:				
	How well you perceive	*How well you understand*	*How well you relate*	*How well you interpret*	*Others?*
Standards are:	Decision about standards was made by:				

The Value System Matrix

The quantity-quality dimension can be related to the three value systems by the *value systems matrix.*

First, let's read the matrix, and then we'll examine a task or two by projecting it on the value systems matrix.

The model is a three dimensional matrix in order to indicate a constant relationship among the three value systems; no one value system ever stands alone, without the others. The relative power of each in deciding which task will be selected and included in a program is a matter of degree determined by the situation and one's philosophical preferences. The other two value systems become subordinates; any task selection has at least one dominating value system and one or two subordinate systems.

The intrinsic system includes all the quantitative dimensions of the tasks; the assigned value system includes the qualitative dimensions determined by rules, aesthetic standards, etc.; the functional value system includes either quantitative, qualitative, or both dimensions depending on what is to be achieved.

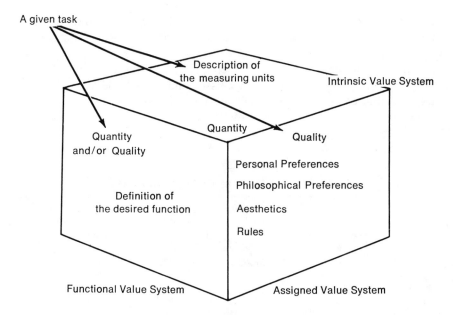

Projection of a Task on the Value System Matrix

Let's start with a task with high visibility: a hook shot in basketball. From each of the three value systems, a statement can be made about this task. For the game of basketball the *dominating* value system is the *functional value system.* The hook shot is used in the game because it serves the function of the game, scoring points by getting the ball through the hoop, and is used by the player because it has functional value for him by bringing him success in the game.

The hook shot also has intrinsic values. Since it is done by jumping off the ground by the thrust of one leg it develops strength, an intrinsic value. This task also requires and develops some degree of coordination, another intrinsic value. And there are other attributes intrinsic to the hook shot, each one of which has quantitative dimensions not necessarily related to the *function* of the shot. But the *intrinsic* values in this case are subordinates, for it really does not matter "how much" strength repetitive hook shots can develop in the take-off leg. The main question is always, "Did the ball get in?"

Similarly, the hook shot has a relationship to the assigned value system: a certain aesthetic value can be assigned to its performance — but, indeed, it is not important how pretty the shot looks: *only* those shots that go into the basket count. Hence, the *assigned* value system is *subordinate* in relation to this task. In fact, the *quality* (which is specific to the assigned value system) of a shot is often, if not always, determined by its quantitative attainment, namely, the number of points! (You can try other task examples in human movement and sports, project each task against the matrix, and find out what happens to it in each value system and how it affects suitability of the task in a program.)

Let's examine the Pythagorean Theorem in geometry, which enables us to calculate the height of a building without directly measuring it: hence its *functional* value. The relationship among the three sides of the triangle expressed by the formula is its *intrinsic* value, its truth and universality. Perhaps it is impossible to decide which is the dominant value system. One could argue either way.

The preference for a particular way of proving this theorem (and there are several dozen solutions) represents the *assigned* value system. Some proofs are more elegant than others. We have all failed a geometry assignment because we did not prove the problem the teacher's way. We perhaps proved it—our proof was functional—we certainly understood the factors intrinsic to that task, but the teacher's assigned value system rejected all correct solutions but his own. (Can you project other tasks in geometry or another branch of mathematics on the matrix and see what happens to them under each value system?)

One more example, from social studies, would be the general topic of U.S. involvement in foreign wars. The task is to establish criteria *for* and *against* participation in foreign wars. Which list to place an item in would seem to depend upon which value system dominates the selection of the criteria. For example, wars have a functional value: to conquer, to dominate. This is true even for so-called defensive wars; in every war there has been a conqueror and a vanquished (whether temporary or permanent). Destruction and death are intrinsic to war. Among the assigned values there are both positive and negative—ranging from claims for war's positive role in biological preservation to the loftiest national ideologies and the most extreme sets of individual morality, from pacifism to cruelty and bestiality.

Now, in the task of setting criteria for and against U.S. participation in foreign wars—or possibly in a particular war or wars—which value system *is* the dominating one? If you assigned this task to your class, how would you handle these value systems? Would the matrix help you?

Individual Program Design by the Matrix

Now let's see how the matrix of value systems and the consideration of quantity and quality affect the design of Individual Programs in various fields. First, examples involving *quantity* as the differentiating dimension of programs in the areas of reading, typing, human movement, and arithmetic skills.

The "simplest" design of a quantitative individual program is one in which the difficulty of a task is affected by increases in one or more quantitative factors in that particular area. A prototype of such an individual program might look like this:

Individual Program: Quantitative

Name _____ Date _____

Grade/Class _____

Subject _____

Value system _____

To the student: [Includes the necessary instruction, comments, and guides pertaining to this program].

Task sequence	Quantitative factor	Task description	Level 1	Level 2	Level 3	Student's comment
1.	(amount,					
2.	time,					
3.	speed,					
4.	etc.)					
5.						

Teacher's comment: _____

_____

_____

Individual Program: Quantitative

Name _____ Date _____

Subject _____ Reading _____ Grade _____

Value system _____ ? _____

To the student: This program is designed for you, for the next three sessions. Start with task #1 and move along at your own pace. Complete as many tasks as you can without neglecting comprehension of content.

Task sequence	Quantitative factor	Task description	Level 1	Level 2	Level 3	Student's comment
1.	Number of pages per session	Read pp. 1–15 (first session)	Read 1–15	Read 1–20	Read 1–30	
2.		Read comments on pp. 215–220	215 220	215 225	215 230	
3.		Read pp. 16–40 (second session)	?	?	?	
4.	(30 min.)	Read mimeographed handouts #1, 2, 3.				

| 5. | (speed) | Read pp. 41–65 (third session) Read comments on pp. 240–250 Read mimeographed handouts #4, 5. Read Ch. 1–2 in the handbook | | | | |

Teacher's comment: _____
_____
_____

Individual Program: Quantitative

Name _____ Date _____

Subject _____ typing-speed improvement _____ Grade _____

Value system _____ functional _____

To the student: The following tasks are arranged for speed improvement. The paragraphs to be typed are those with which you are familiar from previous sessions in which you focused on accuracy.

Task sequence	Quantitative factor	Task description	Level 1	Level 2	Level 3	Student's comment
1.	# of accurate paragraphs per unit of time.	Type paragraph #1 once in 40 seconds (It only counts if it is accurate)	once	twice	three times	
2.	(speed)	Repeat task #1	once	twice	three times	
3.		Type paragraph #2 in 40 seconds	once	twice	three times	
4.		Repeat task #3				
5.		Type paragraph #3 in 40 seconds	once	twice	three times	
6.		Repeat task #5				
7.		Type paragraph #4 in 40 seconds	once	twice	three times	

Teacher's comment: _____
_____
_____

Individual Program: Quantitative

Name _____ Date _____

Subject _____ strength development, abdominal region _____ Grade _____

Value system _____ intrinsic _____

To the student: The following tasks are designed to develop strength in the abdominal region. Start with task #1 and go as far as you can with short intervals (10–15 seconds between tasks).

Task sequence	Quantitative factor	Task description	Level 1	Level 2	Level 3	Student's comment
1.	number of repetitions (amount)	In supine position, legs slightly bent at the knees, sit up	0–5 times	6–10 times	11 and above	
2.		Repeat task #1 (legs straight)	0–5 times	6–10 times	11 on	
3.		Repeat task #1 (straight back)	0–5 times	6–10 times	11 on	
4.		Repeat task #1 (arm above head)	0–5 times	6–10 times	11 on	

Teacher's comment: _____

_____

_____

Individual Program: Quantitative

Name _____ Date _____

Subject _____ number facts – arithmetic _____ Grade _____

Value system _____ ? _____

To the student: The following tasks are arranged to be done during the next few days [specify]. Start from the first and go on through the entire program at your own pace. Check periodically with your teacher for the correct answers. Check as complete only a correct task performance.

Task sequence	Quantitative factor	Task description	Level 1	Level 2	Level 3	Level 4	Level 5	Student's comment
1.	Number of arithmetic exercises performed	Practice writing, in order, the multiplication table	1×1 to 4×4	1×1 to 7×7	1×1 to 10×10	1×1 to 12×12	1×1 to 15×15	
2.		Exercises on pp. 7–10	Ex. 1 to 10	Ex. 1 to 20	Ex. 1 to 30	Ex. 1 to 40	Ex. 1 to 50	
3.		Exercises on pp. 15–20	Ex. 1 to 10	Ex. 1 to 20	Ex. 1 to 30	Ex. 1 to 40	Ex. 1 to 50	

Teacher's comment: _____

_____

_____

Though it is possible and practical to design such programs in many other areas of study, it is important to observe that certain tasks in certain subjects are more suited to a quantitative program than others, and that some are quite unsuited. (Is this a projection of assigned values by the author?) A typing program designed to improve speed (quantitative measure) makes sense: the functional value system can be related to typing.

But a quantitative program in social studies, in which the student were to spout an increasing number of historical facts per unit of time, would be rather ludicrous. So, again, we see the need for insight and for sensitivity to the meaning of task selection and program design.

These samples of quantitative Individual Programs can span a variety of time lengths. An Individual Program can be designed for part of a lesson, a complete lesson, or a series of lessons. The more experienced students become in this style the more able they are to extend their decision making; classes have come close to being self-operating and self-sustaining for a period of weeks by the use of this style.

The quantitative Individual Program can also be designed by introducing variations within each task so that each variation demands a different level of performance — that is, degree of difficulty. A range is offered, by individually varying the factor, in each task. (Such quantitative task factors as number, speed, etc., were discussed under quantitative task differentiation.) Schematically, this design has two dimensions: vertical, a sequence of tasks; and horizontal, levels of performance for each task.

Individual Program: Quantitative Range

Name _____ Date _____
Subject _____ Grade _____
To the student _____

Task sequence	Task description	Level 1	Level 2	Level 3	. . . . .	Quantitative factor
1.						
2.						
3.						
4.						

Such a design with differentiation of both task and performance levels within each task *increases* the possibilities for individualization. Each student has a greater range of choices, and selects the task *and* the level of performance in it best suited to him at that time. An excellent example for our investigation is the push-up: it is visual and lends itself to differentiation.

The push-up has several intrinsic factors which affect performance, such as the initial position of the body and of the arms in relation to the body, the position of the body during the push-up, the speed of the push-up, the number of push-ups, etc. Each can be varied: the body can initially be straight, slightly bent at the hips, or bent to an inverted V, etc.; the arms can be at shoulder width, closer together, or further apart, a little or much; and the number of push-ups can of course be varied. Degree of difficulty can thus be varied in the same task. So, the push-up, a given task in the vertical sequence of tasks, can be varied in specific ways horizontally to accommodate individual differences and possibilities. (It is obvious that one needs to know a subject well in order to do task analysis, determine its factors, and organize the variation into levels of difficulty in the Individual Program.) The quantitative factors in our example are two:

1. Number of repetitions. This will provide a *range* in any activity designed for strength development.
2. Position of the arms. For by kinesiology, the analysis of the mechanics and anatomy of human movement, variations in the degree of difficulty can be mathematically calculated.

Individual Program: Quantitative Range

Name _____ Date _____
Subject _____ strength development _____ Grade _____
To the student: Try performing the activities listed below and circle the quantity of your performance today. You may begin at any level of any of the tasks.

	Task description	Level 1	Level 2	Level 3	Level 4
1.	Push-up; straight body	5, 10, (15), 20 repetitions	Wider arms position 5, (10), 15, 20 rep	Very narrow arms position (5), 10, 15, 20 rep	?
2.					
3.					

For a series of tasks with several performance levels for *each* task, a single-sheet program can guide the student for several sessions. It provides for greater differentiation of both abilities in performance and decision making in both the impact and post-impact sets.

Just as human movement (selected for its high visibility) can serve for individual programs, other subjects can be organized on a range. The designer of a program must analyze the subject to ascertain the various levels of difficulty within it, and then establish the range. In reading, for example, the quantity can serve as a factor of difficulty, just as it serves in human movement:

a. number of pages read.
b. number of pages read per unit of time.
c. number of "difficult" words, etc.

(Can you identify other quantity components that can be planned on a range?)

In mathematics, a range of difficulty can be determined, again, by the number of exercises to be done with or without time limitation. Each exercise can be made easier or more difficult by varying the number of activities to be done with a given exercise: A particular formula, for example, can be applied to various problems, some easier and some harder.

Quality Differentiation

The design of individual programs based on *quality* differentiation will seem similar to the quantitative design. It can appear in the same form for either a single quality of performance or several levels of quality — a range — for each task. Thus, schematically:

Individual Program: Qualitative

Name _____ Date _____
Subject _____ Grade _____
Value system _____
To the student _____

	Task description	Level 1	Level 2	Level 3	Level 4
1.		*poor*	*fair*	*good*	*excellent*
2.					
3.					
4.					

However, it is not as simple as that. The question arises: "How does one determine the quality levels in a given task?" Since statements about quality answer the question "how well?", we must decide what this question *asks* about any task. The question and its answer use the assigned value system. "How well does Ronny read?" "How well does Jesse do social studies?" "How well does Adam do mathematics?" Let's start with these three questions.

When you say that Ronny reads well, which is a qualitative statement, what does it really mean? Does it mean that she can read one hundred pages in fifteen minutes? Does it mean that she can do it consistently — in every reading task? Does it mean that she can answer so many questions about its content? Are these not some of the ways we use to find out "how well" children read? If so, then *none* of these is qualitative! An answer to each of these questions is quantitative. A hundred pages in fifteen minutes represents quantity. It tells you "how much," not "how well." Doing it every time represents quantity. Answering so many questions, again, tells you "how much," not "how well." Yet, quantitative differentiations are used to measure quality.

What, then, will constitute *quality* in reading, for designing an individual program? One can argue that "understanding" must be part of how well one reads. Understanding and reading are two different activities. Ronny can read well (in *some* schools, at least) by quantitative measures alone — speed, number of pages, memory of so many facts — without understanding implications or concepts in the reading. But when we ask, "How well does she understand what she reads?" what kind of answers are we seeking? How well does Ronny understand *what?* Most reading deals with aspects of human existence, what is often called "the human condition": facts, relationships, assumptions, values, aspirations, interpretations, etc. Now, which among these are included in the realm of understanding? *Who* makes decisions about the *kind* of understanding in each one of these facets?

All this is presented to point out the complexity and difficulty of designing reading tasks arranged on a qualitative range. Since many answers to "how well" are reflections of the assigned value system, how does one decide the hierarchy in the range of tasks?

We asked, "How well does Jesse do social studies?" How do we go about answering this question? What are tasks in social studies that represent a range of quality? How do we decide the range? Many issues, perhaps most, in social studies represent insight, interpretations, and statements that reflect the assigned value system. What would the criteria for the range be? Personal preferences and beliefs? Group decision? *Which* group? Let us examine the question, "How well does Adam do mathematics?" What does it mean? Does it mean that he can solve *a* mathematical problem? Two? Many? Any? Does it mean that he can remember formulae? Apply them? Use them? What? How do we design a series of tasks in mathematics that will represent a range of qualitative differentiations?

It seems that we are facing an interesting dilemma. We know that each task has the attributes quantity and quality; we know that these represent different value systems, yet we meet an impasse in the design itself of a range of tasks qualitatively differentiated, in certain subjects. Let's see what happens in music. How do we determine quality in violin playing? What does it mean when we say, "He plays well?" Does it mean that the player adhered to the score and produced the sounds as closely as possible to the composer's notations? Let's assume for a moment that this is what "well" means in playing the violin. How would we know that the player approximated the score? We'll know by *counting* the number of errors that made the playing *not* close to the written score. What kind of errors are there in violin playing? Errors of pitch, interval, bow distribution, etc. — all these are quantitative, not qualitative. They answer the "how much," not the "how well" questions. It is also clear that these dimensions of violin playing represent at times the intrinsic value system and at other times the functional value system.

Yet, we speak about "how well he plays": obviously, we *attribute* a quality to a given performance by some agreed-upon aesthetic standards and qualifications. How do we, then, organize them on a range? Is it perhaps impossible to design a qualitative-range individual program in some fields? Do we leave quality determination as personal, arbitrary, changeable? One solution is to declare clearly the assigned values, their hierarchy, and who chose them. Thus, the range of tasks will be determined by experts who set the standards of quality in the given field, by an individual teacher, or by anyone accepted as an authority in that field.

In fact, let's leave the design of this kind of an individual program to you, the reader. You know your subject; you have achieved a degree of competency in it. See what happens to you and your judgments when you begin to design a quality-hierarchy in it. While doing so, ask yourself the following questions:

1. What *is* quality in my field?
2. What criteria are used for determining it?
3. Did I evolve these criteria?
4. Did I scrutinize and then accept these?
5. Are they really mine? If not,
6. Whose? Why have I accepted them?

We have some ideas now about the theoretical model and operation of the individual program. We know some of its assets and liabilities, some of its projected joys and suspected difficulties. Let us examine the implications of this style of teaching; what does it mean or what might it mean to adjustments or changes in the educational scheme?

Implications of the Individual Program

**Implications of the
Individual Program for
Philosophy of Education**

Regardless of the kind of Individual Program (programmed instruction, contract, I.P.I., quantitative or qualitative programs, etc.) used in a school or a classroom, the teacher who accepts it implies the belief that:

    a.   each student is unique: in physical qualities, social and emotional states, and as a learner.
    b.   each student *can* and *should* learn to make decisions about himself.
    c.   subject matter can and should be individualized.

These beliefs are a matter of educational philosophy, of commitment to a particular role of the individual in learning and, therefore, a commitment to a particular style of teaching, founded on *trust* in the student and his ability to make judgments about himself.

Use of this style implies an educational philosophy that not only *verbalizes* the importance of individual dignity, but also *acts* on this belief. Changes have actually been introduced to affect the life of the student within the walls of the school, because there is *less fear* that the student will make mistakes, and further — perhaps more importantly — *increased trust* that the student can identify and correct them.

**Implications for
Curricular Decisions**

It follows that all curricular decisions and designs must reflect such an educational philosophy that respects individual differences in ability, perception, performance, choice, interest, thinking, feeling, and so on. The curriculum must be changed to suit people, people must not be changed to preserve the curriculum.

This is a difficult demand. Some teachers, administrative personnel, and college professors may feel threatened by such proposals, because patterns that have worked for them and, therefore, are good and right, are being abandoned for the risk of the unknown. This means not knowing what will happen *to them* and what their new role, of making even *fewer* decisions, might bring.

These fears and trepidations are real and understandable; however, a philosophical commitment to greater individualization must endorse risk-taking in new curricular designs, designs so rich, so different, and so variable that every student *actually* finds a place for daily success and frequent reinforcement.

Teachers and administrators confronted with these suggestions respond with a well-conceived — because grounded in experience — system of rationalizations for why these proposals would not, and even *should* not, work. Let us examine this response. Why would a teacher oppose a rational arrangement whereby each student finds a reasonable place, at least during part of the school day? By logical analysis there could be only two reasons:

1. The teacher has never experienced an individualized education. His own education, elementary through college, has been *dominated* by *group principles,* in every aspect of classroom life — group values, procedures, averages, discipline, etc. The individual is *always* secondary to the group. Any teacher thus brought up must have developed the belief (an educational philosophy) that this is the way education *is* and the way it *must* be.
2. The teacher does not know enough about the practice of individualizing. When one does not know, one is often afraid to try, afraid to fail and lose face. Indeed, before a teacher attempts *any* individualized program he must know its concept, structure, process, and consequences, and the implications of individualization within a group.

Unfortunately, there is no substitute for knowledge. Neither gimmicks nor gadgets have yet succeeded in replacing the teacher's understanding. When a teacher understands and experiments with the process of shifting decisions step-by-step, awareness of the process develops, recognition of pitfalls sharpens, and security in remedy and support evolves.

A common error in schools that have made individualizing curricular adjustments is the abruptness and incompleteness of change. Even if philosophical alternatives have been adopted by the faculty, or by individual teachers, curricular change alone is not enough. *Two* more *major* adjustments are needed: a shift in teacher behavior and in anticipated student behavior based on a *clear* set of new expectations.

Remember, the educational experience is a teacher-learner *transaction.* The shift in expected student behavior demands *first* a shift in teacher behavior. A teacher who behaves by *previous* styles cannot bring the individualizing process into bloom. Decisions will conflict, incongruity will develop, and the teaching-learning transaction will be interrupted.

Implications for Discipline and Deviant Behavior

Discipline   Perhaps the most significant implication of the Individual Program is its impact on discipline. Students who have long been involved in individual programs demonstrate:

1. The ability to carry out diverse series of tasks over varying periods of time without constant or direct surveillance by a teacher.
2. Ability to make appropriate impact and post-impact decisions in a great variety of programs in many different activities.
3. Noticeable involvement in the subject matter and in the act of learning.
4. Minimization or complete absence of nonlearning and deviation from the individual programs.
5. Ability to be self-operating for some periods in the teacher's absence.
6. Ability to regulate time, pace, quantity and quality of participation in the process. (*Comment:* Most interesting are the reactions of uninitiated observers who visit classes operating in this style. Three kinds of responses first come from visitors' lips: "How do they [the students] know what to do?" "It is very quiet here!" and "How do you [the teacher] know what's going on?")
7. Greater tolerance of students for their peers. Since tasks are differentiated to ability levels and the resultant achievements are diversified and accepted by the teacher, the tight pressure of competition found in classes operating by group principles is greatly reduced, and each individual student can focus on *his own developmental* process and that of others with more tolerance. The essence of the Individual Program, that "it is all right to be what you are and where you are," is readily accepted and emotionally internalized by students who have been engaged in it over a period of time.

Students show a fundamental change in the very concept of discipline—a change from group discipline, usually dependent on external stimuli and controls, to self-discipline, reflecting competency in making decisions for and about oneself.

These are not merely behavioral *objectives;* they are actually observable after a period of time carefully devoted to the process of shifting decisions step-by-step, nurturing a student who can learn to make decisions. Every decision made by the student is one decision fewer to be made by the teacher and a step closer to a state of independence.

Deviant behavior   Both theoretically and operationally, this style provides for individual decisions in two sets of the anatomy of an Individual Program. Therefore, inability or unwillingness to make a decision will *theoretically* constitute deviant behavior. (A gentle warning to the teacher who is a novice in the individualizing process: Perhaps it should be stated that inability or unwillingness to make a decision may constitute *temporary deviant behavior.*)

Introduction of the Individual Program to classes accustomed to other styles of teaching — particularly the Command Style — requires time for adjustment, especially individual adjustment. Although the theory suggests that students wish to and can make decisions, the reality of the classroom (or the camp, the club, or any other group organization) indicates great differences in the *readiness* to make decisions.

Unreadiness is emotional rather than cognitive. Over the years, students, regardless of age, have learned (primarily under the Command Style) that in school it is *not safe* to make decisions on their own. When asked to do so in regard to specific subjects they hesitate, and sometimes refuse. They are not sure of the consequences. A period of silence and inactivity is quite common after introduction of the idea and procedures of the Individual Program. Students generally understand the idea and can follow the procedures, but these two are apparently insufficient. They also need to *feel* that their new behavior of making individual decisions will be accepted and rewarded, and certainly not rejected or reprimanded. This emotional readiness requires time.

Silence and inactivity must not always be interpreted by the teacher as deviant behavior. Diverse individuals need different lengths of time to overcome *inhibitions* inculcated in them for some years by other styles of teaching. In fact, this situation can test the teacher's own emotional readiness to accept diversity of readiness among his students. Some teachers fail this test; their own inhibitions and hang-ups overpower sensitivity to the need for time, which usually results in the following teacher behaviors:

1. Identifying the students as deviant behavers
2. Condemning them for their deviant behavior
3. Seeking ways to retaliate (in order to maintain the teacher's equilibrium)
4. Retaliation by reprimanding the students
5. Retaliation by condemning and rejecting this style of teaching
6. Failure to conduct the Individual Program with its benefits to the students (and teacher)
7. Retreat to other styles that are less threatening to the emotional safety of the teacher.

Can you think of what you will do if your class does not glide easily into perfect execution of the Individual Program? Will you get angry? Will you rationalize? Will you reject?

**Implications for Systems
of Reward and Reprimand
and Verbal Behavior**

Reprimand   From everything said above about the need some students will have for adjustment time, it should be clear that a teacher *must not rush* to invoke the system of reprimands—certainly not those used for the Command Style, or perhaps for any other styles. The principal difference is that in the Command Style students are prohibited from doing things on their own, and, here, students have no choice but to do just that. Any deviation from these, almost polar, positions cannot be treated in the same way.

In fact, there may be no reprimand system appropriate to this style, since a teacher cannot force a student to participate in individual decision making. The only hazard (for the student) is that by not participating in the individual program the student may lag behind the class in knowledge, experience, skill, etc. A needed word of caution: Because the student knows that the teacher cannot enforce this style, again patience is needed. Do not rush to reprimand. Instead, get more information about the refusal to participate. Ask the student such questions as: "Are all the tasks in the program clearly presented?" or "Was I clear when I explained the tasks?" or "Would you like me to demonstrate this task again?" All this must be done individually, never in a group. It is important to refrain from moralizing statements and from questions that imply recrimination. Either of these tends to reduce potential communication, and often subverts the goals of this style. To refrain from such verbal behavior is suggested not from kindliness but because it is important to recruit the complete trust of the student if this style is to be employed. Any hesitation or delay by the student must be treated in a manner which provides the student with a way out, a way to save face—particularly in front of those peers who seem to be already involved in their own individual programs. Moralizing and recrimination do not allow this; often they close the door; they serve as last statements against which the student *must* retaliate. Retaliatory techniques are varied and plentiful: withdrawal, ridicule, accusation, and so on. When students retaliate the teacher must respond—often with what he thinks should be stronger retaliation—and the vicious cycle has begun.

Reward   Execution of the individual program is a reward in itself, because the student has achieved something on his own. Often the student feels self-rewarded and self-motivated when he knows he has progressed from task to task or from one level to another—quantitatively, qualitatively, or both. This motivation to continue brings about further involvement in the Individual Program, which often results in additional progress and, again, self-reward.

This chain of events is rather intriguing. So far on the spectrum this is the only style in which assessment is not performed by an outsider. It is a new condition of heightened privacy. One evaluates what one has done; nobody else knows or intervenes. Indeed, a new learning condition. Some students will need a considerable amount of time to adjust to this, particularly those who have been motivated to learn primarily by external rewards.

In relation to the reward system, the teacher, the provider of external rewards, has a unique opportunity in this style. He has ample time (always a precious commodity in teaching) for communication with individual students. This communication can emphasize acknowledgement of the student's achievement. While the student is engaged in specific task-evaluation as prescribed in the program, the teacher is able to observe performance and achievement and to deliver general or specific statements of approval.

Even if a critical, corrective statement must be made, when done individually, in private, for the purpose of helping and supporting, to the student it will be a kind of reward, because unlike previous styles of teaching, this style provides the time and the behavioral climate for intimate contact between student and teacher. This kind of immediacy, privacy, and attentiveness is very gratifying to most students. It makes them feel alive, noted, important, a part of an evolving process of things happening, it helps them feel that they can learn—their own way and for their own growth.

**Implications for the
Development Channels**

Where is the student who is in this kind of Individual Program on the developmental channels?

Theoretical Limits Concept

Minimum ←		*→ Maximum*
Physical Development		X
Social Development	X	
Emotional Development		X
Intellectual Development	X	

The individual program provides for much independence in decisions about participation in physical involvement. The X can be placed close to maximum.

The X on the social development channel is placed toward minimum because theoretically and operationally the Individual Program involves self-participation, self-involvement, and self-performance. Because it is intrinsic to this style that things are done by oneself, there is virtually no opportunity to socialize.

The X on the emotional developmental channel was placed towards maximum because it is assumed that any student who can function alone and make a series of decisions about himself and his performance in a subject has strong emotional security. Students who are not as secure about their own performance and decisions are more *dependent* on the teacher's chain of decisions and cannot function alone in the individual program. They constantly need a teacher to tell them what to do, and when and how to do it, etc. Such conduct reflects emotional rather than cognitive dependency.

The X on the intellectual developmental channel is also placed more toward the minimum pole, because it is intrinsic to this style that the *kind* of decisions that the student makes in this style require only a limited involvement in cognitive operation. Evaluation decisions that come from comparing and contrasting and judging results against criteria involve cognitive activity, but only a rather moderate amount.

Have you any other observations about this style? Can you identify any hazards? Hazards to whom—the students? the teacher? the school? Have you experienced other implications? other advantages? Do you have other observations concerning the developmental channels?

7 Guided Discovery

One of the most striking phenomena about the spectrum up to this point is that, for any subject, the X on the intellectual channel is dragging, is still near minimum. It is striking for two reasons:

1. Since we have traveled quite a distance from the Command Style, its intrinsic restrictions on the student should have been dissipated by now. This may be true of the other developmental channels, but not of the intellectual channel.
2. Certain subjects in school have typically been categorized as "intellectual experiences" (math, physics, literature, etc.). Indeed they are, but only at certain times, and, for all styles so far, only on the surface.

It seems audacious to suggest that these subjects are only "part time" intellectual activities, but analysis of cognitive operations applied to the teaching styles discussed thus far will reveal that some or many of the cognitive operations are not invoked in teaching.

Cognitive operations are the mental activities that cognitive psychologists have derived from their research and theoretical work. Some of these operations are:

1. Recognizing data
2. Analyzing
3. Synthesizing
4. Comparing and contrasting
5. Drawing conclusions
6. Hypothesizing
7. Memorizing
8. Inquiring
9. Extrapolating
10. Intuiting
11. Inventing

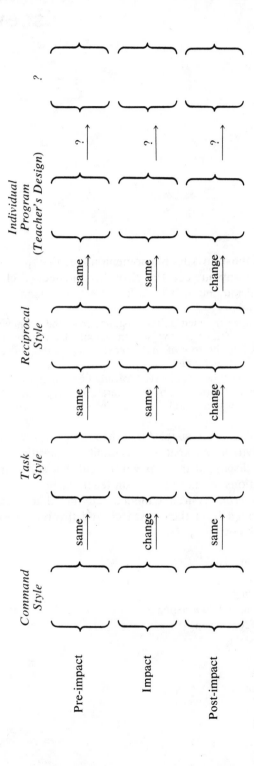

12. Discovering
13. Many others

That all of us are capable of these activities is known, as are some of their consequences. But, so far in the spectrum, if any of these operations have been called upon, it has been randomly, by chance. What must a teacher *do* in order to evoke these cognitive operations *deliberately?* Which style of teaching can accomplish this?

An examination of the relationships between the styles thus far discussed and the list of cognitive operations makes clear that these styles rarely if ever call upon some of these operations, and certainly provide no opportunity to develop them. As an extreme example, let us examine the relationship between the Command Style and these operations.

The Command Style

Cognitive operation	*Deliberately invoked*	*Not invoked*	*May appear independently*
Recognizing data	X		
Analyzing		X	X
Synthesizing		X	X
Comparing and contrasting		X	X
Drawing conclusions		X	X
Hypothesizing		X	X
Memorizing	X		
Inquiring	sometimes	X	X
Inventing		X	X
Discovering		X	X

Many of these cognitive operations *cannot* be deliberately invoked by the Command Style because their essence is to doubt, to disturb, to find alternatives. This contradicts the status quo and singularity of purpose represented in the Command Style; the consequences of these cognitive operations might be counter to the teacher's decisions. For example, when a geometry teacher using the Command Style teaches a class a way of proving a particular problem, he has already made *every* decision about the problem, its components, relationships, conclusions, etc. All the student must do is somehow "understand" and remember the teacher's presentation: a *minimal* number of cognitive operations. When the teacher *asks* a question which *shows* the connection between the given data and the first step toward solution, the student *does not* ask it, but only repeats it. When the teacher *shows* the relationship between an axiom and the solution of the problem the student *is not* involved in discovering relationships; he merely receives and repeats what the teacher said. When the teacher draws the conclusions from the data and states the proof, the student *is not* engaged in drawing conclusions; he merely repeats the conclusions drawn by the teacher. (Such examples can be cited in all subjects. Can you identify in your field and in your teaching which cognitive operations are frequently engaged? Which ones are only presumed to exist due to the student's imitation of what you have done?)

It is not the subject matter, it is the style of teaching that brings about engagement in the variety of cognitive operations. The question remains: Which style will do so? What is it that the teacher must do or not do, say or not say, to elicit specific cognitive behaviors *regardless* of subject matter?

The realization that thus far on the spectrum many cognitive operations have not been called for or at best have been minimally employed suggests a theoretical barrier on the spectrum—a *cognitive barrier:* symbolically a line of demarcation or point of transition from styles of lower cognitive power to those of higher cognitive power. The distance between Command Style and the cognitive barrier can be considered the state of *cognitive acquiescence,* in which students tacitly accept the decrees of others—schematically:

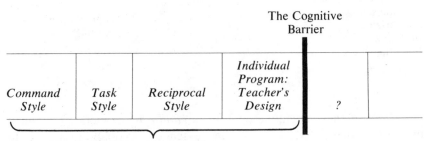

The State of Cognitive Acquiescence

We can rephrase our previous question and ask now: How do we break through the cognitive barrier, from cognitive acquiescence to cognitive involvement?

In his work on cognitive dissonance, Leon Festinger (16) suggests that just as certain biological phenomena serve as a physical disturbance or irritation (hunger, for example), so it is in the mind: certain things disturb or irritate the mind and put it in a special state: *cognitive dissonance.* Just as hunger can be removed by eating, Festinger suggests that cognitive dissonance can be removed by doing something about the original cause of the irritation. The dissonance can be dealt with directly through activity. Psychoanalytically oriented theoreticians and practitioners insist that often dissonance is treated by suppressing it to the unconscious; so:

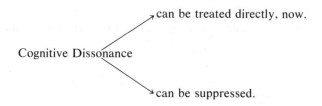

Cognitive Dissonance

can be treated directly, now.

can be suppressed.

In our search for a style of teaching that will help us cross the cognitive barrier, the theory of cognitive dissonance and its direct action component becomes very helpful. If, indeed, cognitive dissonance is an irritation that must be relieved at its source — that is, by solving the problem that bothers the mind — let us develop ways of *creating* this cognitive dissonance *deliberately!* If we could create sequences of dissonances, the student would have two choices — to ignore the dissonance (suppress it) or do something about it. Doing something about removing the dissonance calls for the use of one or more cognitive operations.

The first step is to create dissonance:

Step 1	*Step 2*	
Creating cognitive dissonance ⟶	? ⟶	?

This cognitive dissonance will be relieved when the created problem has been solved and cognitive consonance is achieved. You might expect Step 2 to be: the solution. It is not — because *no solution* is possible without a previous step of *seeking, inquiring.*

No matter how long it takes — a few minutes, a month or a flash of instantaneous discovery — a solution is always preceded by inquiry. So the three-step model is:

Step 1	*Step 2*	*Step 3*
Creating cognitive dissonance ⟶	Inquiry ⟶	Solution: cognitive consonance

A solution is always a result of previous inquiry, while inquiry is always a result of previous dissonance: without dissonance there is no need to inquire; without inquiry there is no solution. These three steps are congruent with the relationship of stimulus–mediation–response, spoken of by cognitive psychologists. This S–M–R model suggests that between the stimulus and the response there is a phase of mediation; a phase of particular kinds of cognitive operations that produce particular kinds of responses. The congruence between these two models looks like this:

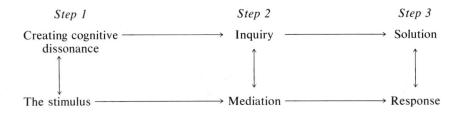

The stimuli may vary, each producing a different kind of mediation activity (the various cognitive operations) resulting in a different response (solution), but all must exist.

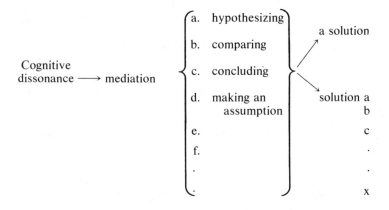

This sequence can be expressed in *operational* terms, which will guide the teacher in the execution of daily sessions, but which require particular teaching behavior designs:

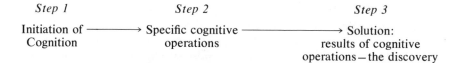

Step 1   *Step 2*   *Step 3*

Initiation of ⟶ Specific cognitive ⟶ Solution:
Cognition   operations   results of cognitive
       operations — the discovery

Schematically, the three congruent sets are:

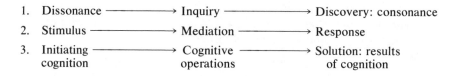

1. Dissonance ⟶ Inquiry ⟶ Discovery: consonance
2. Stimulus ⟶ Mediation ⟶ Response
3. Initiating ⟶ Cognitive ⟶ Solution: results
     cognition   operations   of cognition

All three sets are the same: The first is the theory of the relationship, the second is a psychological model, and the third is an operational guide.

We can ask the following questions about this three-phase model:

1. What kinds of stimuli will, in fact, lead to inquiry?
2. Is it possible, in a given subject, to identify a specific stimulus or group of them that will create cognitive dissonance?
3. How do we identify the *specific* stimulus that will evoke a *specific* cognitive operation? Will any stimulus induce any operation? Suppose we want the student to compare and contrast — how do we *initiate* it, and maintain it?
4. What teaching style must (or can) be used so that our behavior not only initiates and maintains a given cognitive process (by the learner) but will also lead to solution and achieve consonance?
5. Does the kind of solution known or anticipated determine the *kind* of initiation and the *kind* of inquiry?
6. What is the preferable *verbal behavior* for the initiation phase?
7. What verbal behavior will keep the student on course? And what will cause deviation or even destruction of the desired process?
8. What kinds of actions will be congruent with the desired verbal behavior? Will certain actions inhibit, curtail, or abolish the process desired?
9. How does all this apply to the teaching of chemistry, mathematics, literature, music, human movement, physics, art, and so on?

In order to cross the cognitive barrier it is necessary to identify, design, and use teaching styles that employ these three phases in a deliberate manner. The first style of teaching past the barrier is *Guided Discovery*. In this style, the teacher guides the student through small, sequential discoveries until he discovers the *focus,* the goal, that the teacher has selected: The student is presented with a sequence of questions (or clues) so meticulously arranged that the student *always* discovers the correct response until the target (the focus) is reached.

This process represents the concept of *converging thinking* (Katona, 29), whereby thinking is directed toward a particular target—a bit of information, an idea, a principle. In Guided Discovery converging thinking is composed of "small" discoveries—discoveries by and for the learner at that moment. They need not be earthshaking; they are significant for the person engaged in the act of discovery (12).

The mathematician Polya (36) expounded on the beauty and excitement of discovery and the heuristic process:

> A great discovery solves a great problem but there is a grain of discovery in the solution of any problem. Your problem may be modest, but if it challenges your curiosity and brings into play your inventive faculties, and if you solve it by your own means, you may experience the tension and enjoy the triumph of discovery. Such experiences at a susceptible age may create a taste for mental work and leave their imprint on mind and character for a lifetime.

In order to create and maintain a heuristic climate the teacher must make several behavioral adjustments. First, the teacher must *never tell the answer!* The instant an answer is given to a student the process of cognitive dissonance → inquiry → discovery ceases.

The second requirement is a *linguistic adjustment:* instead of declarative statements, which tend to be final statements, closed situations, one shifts to questions. A question connotes openness, a possibility for a further step. (True, some questions *elicit* final statements, but this doesn't necessarily violate the *spirit* of questioning behavior.)

For the student, a question may have a different connotation from that of a declarative statement, and a different set of actions may occur:

1. The student learns that the teacher is interested in what he has to say.
2. He learns that he is *expected* to give an answer.
3. To be able to give an answer requires an understanding of the question. One must pay attention in order to hear and understand the question.
4. If the question is relevant (we shall return later to the issue of relevancy) then the student is *beginning* to be *actively* involved with the teacher.
5. This involvement is usually a result of the cognitive dissonance created by the question.
6. The cognitive process has begun. The student now *must* pursue the answer.

It is fascinating to watch a class (or individuals) engage in this process of sequential discoveries when the teacher only asks questions and never gives answers.

One feeling that students demonstrate at times during guided discovery is frustration. It usually results from the teacher's refusal to give answers, but it may also result from improper timing, pacing, or the kind of questions asked. Frustration experienced during Guided Discovery often leads to withdrawal from the process. On the other hand, a well-designed sequence of questions can create excitement and intellectual dynamism in almost any class. Timing, pacing, and proper design come with experience.

It is safe to say that Guided Discovery is probably the hardest style to master. It imposes the greatest demands on the teacher, who must know the learner's behavior and the structure of the subject matter, and must be extremely adept at the style of teaching itself. A teacher can be effective in other styles at various levels of competency in them, but in Guided Discovery a teacher cannot be effective at all unless he is very competent in this style.

The next adjustment needed is within the affective domain: Wait for the answer; it will come; wait some more. Waiting requires the cultivation of patience. Many teachers have not learned to wait. Once one understands its undisputed value in the development and evolution of a discovery process one can learn to wait.

Not waiting, and supplying the answer at any given point during the sequence of discoveries, may result in:

a. Reducing the excitement of discovery
b. Reducing the trust developed by the student
c. Reducing the interest caused by the dissonance
d. Terminating the very process that has been put in motion.

Wait for the answers!

(I can remember moments of waiting while shooting the TV series "Shape-Up," a CBS–Rutgers University venture. I used Guided Discovery many times in the teaching of concepts, principles, relationships, and so on. At times, the waiting must have taken 20 or 30 seconds or perhaps longer. In front of three TV cameras it is a hell of a long time. I can remember sweating, and cameramen getting alarmed that something had gone wrong. But I waited. I would not dare interrupt those seconds of total concentration by children seeking answers. I would not dare deprive the children of that joyful moment of discovery. During seven years of weekly programs, I never interrupted them. And they never disappointed me, or themselves. They always made their discoveries, because I had learned to wait.)

One more adjustment has to be made by the teacher: he must learn to always accept and frequently reinforce. Guided Discovery calls for a carefully designed sequence of questions (stimuli) if correct answers (responses) are to ensue; the more appropriate the question, the more accurate the answers and the more gratifying is the experience to students. They *know* that they are producing appropriate responses, they know that they are moving along a successful course.

Nevertheless, the teacher needs to give reinforcement, because, periodically delivered, it is very reassuring to students. They need to feel that their answers and solutions are accepted by the teacher.

Even an erroneous response can be corrected without destroying acceptance. Remember that students will engage in this process only if it is worthwhile for *them,* which it will be if they are excited about their findings and emotionally comfortable as a result of the teacher's acceptance. It is necessary at times, in order to preserve the integrity of the students and the process, to retrace or change the question or clue, as when an excessive pause indicates an impasse, or when the response is tangential. This happens to every teacher who uses Guided Discovery; not all sequential questions are perfect. This kind of obstacle can be removed by saying to the students, "My question was not clear. Let me try this one . . . ," or anything else in this spirit. Additional questions, corrected questions, or clues are legitimate and necessary to keep the process moving toward the target.

With more experience in Guided Discovery, the teacher will reduce the number of questions that lead to tangential responses. It is possible, however, in certain subjects to develop some sessions that are "perfect" and error-proof. Guided Discovery can be schematized as a ladder or a series of steps:

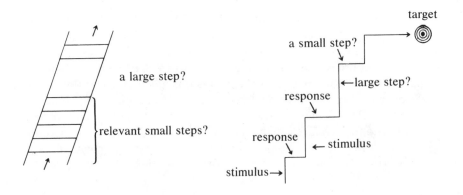

Let's first discuss the Anatomy of Guided Discovery and then the problems of design.

The Anatomy of Guided Discovery

The most significant change that Guided Discovery makes from previous styles is that for the first time the *student makes decisions about subject matter* (during the impact set). These are not pre-impact decisions about what subject matter is to be learned (still the teacher's decision), but about specifics of the subject matter. Even these are decisions that coincide with those the teacher would have made: the sequence of discoveries by the student *are* the subject matter details. Every successful question in the sequence produces another particle of the subject matter. These are the details that would appear if taught by any other style, but here they are discovered by the student.

Pre-Impact Decisions

The teacher's major responsibility in the pre-impact set is to design the questions (or clues) that will lead the student to the focus, or target, determined by the teacher. A focus to be discovered by the student can be a fact, a series of facts, a particular relationship, concept, principle, formula, structure, rule, or anything else in the structure of the subject matter. The teacher must make decisions about several aspects of the guided-discovery process:

a. The *focus*
b. The initial phase: the *first* step
c. The *sequence* of questions or clues
d. The *size* of the step (which determines the pace of the process)

The rest of the decisions in the pre-impact set can be made as before to accommodate the flow of the lesson.

Impact Decisions

The execution phase of Guided Discovery is the test of the sequence design. The flow of the process—from step to step—will indicate the appropriateness of the questions. Theoretically, Guided Discovery is flawless; it leads the learner from the first step to the target with no hitches, no tangents. This, of course, is rare; there are almost always some flaws. Students differ in the way they perceive the same question and in the way they think, so that periodically there is a need to adjust the flow of the process.

Since, by definition, students make decisions about the specifics of subject matter in the impact set of this style, there is always a possibility that someone in the class will make an inappropriate decision—one which does not move toward the target, a tangential response or, indeed, a wrong one.

When this occurs, the teacher needs to make an *adjustment decision*. But first and foremost the teacher must acknowledge the response. The difficulty here is this: How do you acknowledge a wrong response? How do you indicate to the student that the response is not correct without interrupting the flow of the discovery process? It is a question of preference; what is more important, the student's comfortable feelings about his answer or the flow of the process itself?

The teacher is confronted with *unique* moments in this style and decisions must be made about such delicate situations. Some might argue this point; to them, this kind of sensitivity is exaggerated. Those who have conducted sessions by Guided Discovery, particularly with a group, know how *contagious* behavior can be—and in two directions: complete silence or dynamic participation. When individual students (the bold ones) begin to overtly respond other students *watch*, in order to determine *how safe* it is to participate in this seemingly open-ended experience. And from their observations they make their *decisions about participation*. (A teacher can never force a student to participate in Guided Discovery: by definition it will cease to be this style.) If they feel the climate of safety and of acceptability they will join in. But it takes time and sensitivity.

At times, this joining-in engulfs the entire class and students get swept up with the process *and* the product: the accomplishment of the task, the understanding of the concept, the realization of a theory. On the other hand, when a teacher's behavior, by word or gesture, connotes rejection, the participating student will be more cautious about responding. Those students who watch have noticed. If this kind of teaching behavior is frequent students will withdraw from active involvement, silence will spread in the room, cool faces will be staring at the teacher, and gloom will prevail. Nothing happens; the teacher's questions go unheeded, the clues evoke no response: the process is doomed.

It is always the teacher who is the cause of failure in Guided Discovery, never the student. Perhaps we can say that in this style, the decisions made during the impact set are most crucial, more crucial than in any previous style. It is the delicate nature of the on-going transaction between the teacher and the student that requires this kind of sensitivity about the decisions.

A word about adjustment decisions: to an inappropriate response (mainly a tangential answer) the teacher might say: "I can see your point, does it follow from our previous step?" or "Have you examined your answer?" There must be other ways of conveying to the student that his participation is welcome and yet the response needs to be reconsidered, restated, or refined.

A teacher and a class developing experiences in this process will soon reach a state of marvelous interplay of decisions; interplay which reflects mutual trust, mutual curiosity, and mutual joy in sharing the drama of cognitive evolution.

Post-Impact Decisions

The post-impact decisions are *interwoven* with the impact decisions. The very process of Guided Discovery requires that a post-impact decision be made after *every* impact execution. Every stimulus (reflecting the pre-impact decision) is followed by a response (student's impact decision) which in turn is followed by "on the spot" evaluation (teacher's post-impact decision) before the next stimulus can be emitted. This cycle is very precise and its integrity is necessary for the survival of the process.

The Design of Guided Discovery

The theory of Guided Discovery is interesting and exciting; research abounds in proof of its value and efficacy. One of the difficulties, though, is the design itself. The question is: how does one go about designing the appropriate steps that will lead to the target? What must a teacher *know* in order to design such a process? As previously stated, the following pre-impact decisions must be made:

a. Decision about the *focus* and the setting of the scene
b. Decision about the *initial* phase — the *first* step
c. Decision about the *sequence* of questions
d. Decision about the *size* of each step

a. Decision about the focus   A *focus* in this context means a *specific* objective of the lesson. Without it there can be no Guided Discovery. One cannot flounder or explore "freely" in *this* style. Since

Guided Discovery is the operational design reflecting *converging thinking,* the focus of convergence must be identified in advance. A focus of a lesson can be many things:

  i. The facts in a given subject: those elements, bits of information, intrinsic to the structure of the subject matter. For example, the variety of sounds (notes) in music are the "facts" of a musical composition. Without them there is no composition. Numbers are the "facts" of arithmetic. Certain events are the "facts" of a particular historical period. Certain movements are the "facts" of a given sport.

  This means that a successful Guided Discovery process will *result* in the *discovery* of the fact (or facts) chosen as a focus; that fact and no other, no peripheral data, no additional information.

  ii. A relationship among facts. Within any aggregation of facts in any subject matter there are a variety of relationships. A *particular relationship* can serve as a focus for Guided Discovery. For example: there is a relationship between the American and the French revolutions which can be discovered by students if the process is successfully guided by the teacher. . . . There may even be several relationships between the two revolutions. Each such relationship can be a focus of a single episode in Guided Discovery—for discovery of *one* particular relationship, since in converging thinking the discovery of alternative relationships must be avoided. In mechanics, there are particular relationships among force, resistance, and position of the fulcrum. These relationships determine the existence of the three classes of levers. These relationships (or one of them) can serve as a focus for discovery. Can you think of relationships which exist in your field that can serve as a focus?

  iii. Concepts can serve as a focus. Every subject is bound together by concepts, by sets of concepts—for example, the concept of acceleration in physics; the concept of a governing body in social studies; the concept of offense in basketball.

  iv. A particular behavior can serve as a focus. If you want your students to learn to draw conclusions based on analysis of data, a lesson can be designed in which the focus is learning the cognitive behavior, the *act* of drawing conclusions. (This focus, by the way, is fascinating to use with young children. While learning to draw conclusions children usually reveal prejudices, inhibitions, reliance on clichés, fuzzy thinking, and many more cognitive substitutes, as well as clear thinking.) In the same manner other cognitive behaviors can serve as focii for lessons in guided discovery.

  V. Anything else? Actually, anything can serve as a focus. The important point is that a decision about a focus must be made so that the design can adhere to it. You must know where you are going before you can get there. A focus decision provides a *direction* for the process of Guided Discovery.

b. Decision about the initial phase   One of the most difficult and challenging questions is: "How do we start?" What is our first question to the student? (Polya, 36) Assuming the establishment of a clear focus, which is always some distance away, how do we begin? What is the first step that will set the process on its right course and "guarantee" reaching the target in a minimum of steps (perhaps the criterion of an efficient Guided Discovery)?

Suppose we wanted to teach a child the *concept* of factoring numbers, what would be our first question? Would you ask the child: "How do we factor numbers?" The chances are that the child would not know the meaning of the word or the operation of factoring. So, what would you ask instead? What is it that we want to accomplish? We want the child to discover that each number is composed of other numbers and that this composition is specific and has an order. So, let's take one facet at a time and follow this sequence:

Question 1:   Which number is greater – 10 or 6?
Anticipated answer: 10 is greater.
Teacher's response: Yes!
Question 2:   How much greater?
Anticipated answer: Greater by 4.
Teacher's response: Good.
Question 3:   If you wanted to make 6 grow and become 10 what must you do?
Anticipated answer: I add 4.
Teacher's response: Yes.
Question 4:   So, we can say that actually number 10 is made up of – what?
Anticipated answer: 6 and 4.
Teacher's response: Correct.
Question 5:   Suppose we used 8 instead of 6 – what then?
Anticipated answer: Then we'll have to add only 2.
Question 6:   Then 10 can also be made up of what?
Anticipated answer: 8 and 2.
Question 7:   Which is the greatest number we can use for this game and still have 10?
Anticipated answer: $10 + 0 = 10$.
Teacher's response: Right!
Question 8:   What would be the next greatest number?
Anticipated answer: $9 + 1$.
Question 9:   What are the pairs of numbers that make up 10, starting from the largest number first in the pair, and ending with the smallest?
Anticipated answer: $10 + 0$; $9 + 1$; $8 + 2$; $7 + 3$; . . . ; $0 + 10$
Teacher's response: Excellent!
Question 10:   Can this be done with a number other than 10?
Anticipated answer: Yes!

Question 11: Would you select a number?
Anticipated answer: 15! (just as an example)
Question 12: Can you do the same with number 15?
Anticipated answer: Yes. $15 + 0$; $14 + 1$; $13 + 2$; $12 + 3$; . . . ; $0 + 15$.
Question 13: What can we say now about numbers?
Anticipated answer: We can say that they are a combination of pairs of smaller numbers [or any answer similar to this].

So you see that the first question has great relevance to the correct direction of this process. (In the example offered there may be other "first questions" that might conduct the process toward its end.)

When you design a sequence, test with one person only — any person. If you get stuck, check your first question, see where it led you and make an adjustment.

An important aspect of the initial phase of guided discovery besides the first question is creating an environment, physical or intellectual, that can serve as an initial motivation and can draw concentration to the topic. There are many possibilities:

i. A general statement or question. "All ball games consist of offense and defense." "Some of the most striking events in human development occurred in the last century." "Did you know that muscles can only pull? They never push!" Such remarks or questions draw attention to the general area of inquiry.

ii. A particular physical setting. This might include models, maps, charts, pictures, tools, instruments, etc., arranged or displayed to draw attention, only to set the scene for the discovery process.

iii. Involvement of people in an activity. On one of the TV programs previously mentioned the focus was the social concepts of cooperation and competition. The scene was set by having one group of children do something *together* (carrying a heavy load across the room) and the other group do something *against* others (tug-of-war). These activities led to a discovery and discussion of the social phenomena and the behavioral components of each. (The children were nine years old.)

If we see Guided Discovery as a process of convergent thinking,

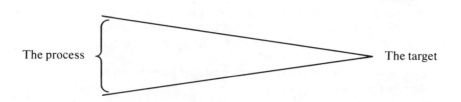

The process   The target

we can say the wide end is the general area of inquiry; setting the scene will be there and will slowly narrow — no deviations, no distractions — until the target is reached.

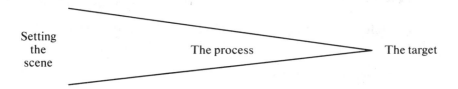

Setting the scene   The process   The target

To set the scene is not always necessary but is helpful. It creates expectancy and sets limits which help focus and concentrate.

    c. Decision about the sequence   It should be clear by now that a major aspect of the design is the *sequence*. A definite order is needed in any design of Guided Discovery; perhaps several parallel designs could lead to the same desired target, but each one must adhere to a particular sequence. Certain questions must precede others and some must follow others to produce the desired results. Any step directly relates to the response to the *previous* step. Recall the factoring example: the first step was a question: "What is the difference between 10 and 6?" This was to elicit the response: "10 is larger," which led to: "How much larger?" and so on. So, theoretically for this sequence each question follows the response to the previous one. To argue that the first question could have elicited different responses, such as: 10 and 6 look different or sound different, and so on, does not change the principle of sequence design. The response, "They look different" would still determine the subsequent question, designed to bring the learner onto a number-concept path ("10 is larger"). It means that additional steps are needed — *or* that the first question *is not* the "best" for this sequence. (Would you care to design another question to initiate the process along the proper path and yet not give away the answer?)

    Another way of designing the sequence is by "going backward." First, one designs the *last* step. Since the focus is known, there must be a way of identifying the last question that will produce an answer on target:

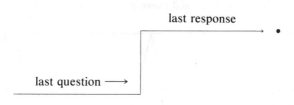

last response

last question ⟶

From this step you move to the one before, and so on until you get to the first step. This is a procedure for the design. Now, operationally, you move forward, starting with the first step and on along the sequence. The first step can be determined by finding out where the student is along the sequence of questions.

d. Decisions about the size of the step   These depend upon two factors:

1. The subject and its focus
2. The learner's sophistication

It is possible, of course, to design a sequence with steps so small that the sequence can theoretically "fit" all students (programmed learning materials; teaching machines; and the like. Some of these are forms of Guided Discovery). However, a teacher who is developing experiences in this style will also learn to adjust step size when teaching groups containing different levels of linguistic and cognitive sophistication.

Examples of Lessons in Guided Discovery

1. Focus: Discovering the three classes of levers   and the roles of the axis, the force arm, and the resistance arm in the operation of the lever in each class.

Setting the scene: (needed equipment) meter-stick, balancing stand, two equal weights (50 grams), two weight hangers, string.

Step 1:   Balance the meter-stick on the balancing stand. (This step can also be considered as part of the scene-setting.)

Step 2:   Ask, "How can we upset the equilibrium, or balance?"

Anticipated answer: "Push one side down or up!" ("Correct!")

Step 3:   Ask, "Can we do the same by use of weights?"

Anticipated answer: (Usually, a student volunteers to place a weight on one side of the meter-stick.) ("Good!")

Step 4:   Ask, "Can you balance the seesaw now?"

Anticipated answer: (Another student will place the other weight on the other side of the meter-stick and move it around until the stick balances.)

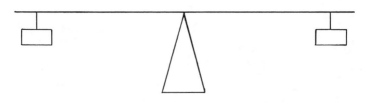

Step 5: Ask, "What factors maintain the balance?"

Anticipated answer: "Equal weight at equal distances from the axis."

Step 6: Ask, "Which factor can we change now to upset the balance?"

Anticipated answer: "The distance of either weight from the axis." (One of the students is asked to do it by moving one of the weights.)

Step 7: Ask, "How far can you move it?"

Anticipated answer: "To the end of the meter-stick."

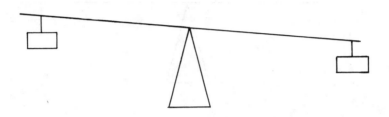

Step 8: Ask, "Is this the maximum distance possible between the end-stick weight and the axis?"

Anticipated answer: "No; it is possible to move the axis further."

Step 9: Ask, "Would you do it, please?"

Anticipated answer: (A student will move the meter-stick so the axis is now at the opposite end from the last-moved weight.)

Step 10: "Now could you use the equipment to balance the stick?"

Anticipated answer: (Most frequently students discover the following solution: they put the string around the stick between the weight and the axis and slowly pull the stick up until it balances in the horizontal position.

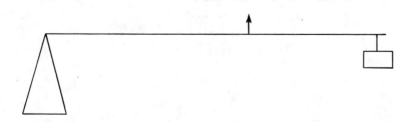

Step 11: "Among the axis, the weight, and the taut string, what kinds of balanced arrangements have we thus far?"

Anticipated answer:

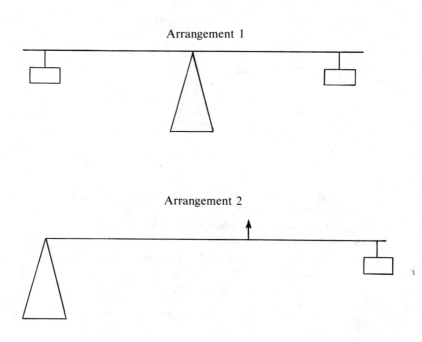

Arrangement 1

Arrangement 2

Step 12: "Look at the second arrangement. Is it possible to change any factors and have a new balanced arrangement?"

Anticipated answer: (After, possibly, a short pause, the following will be offered):

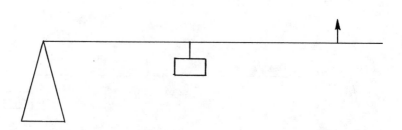

Step 13: "These are the three—and the only—possible arrangements of levers and factors of axis, weight, and force:"

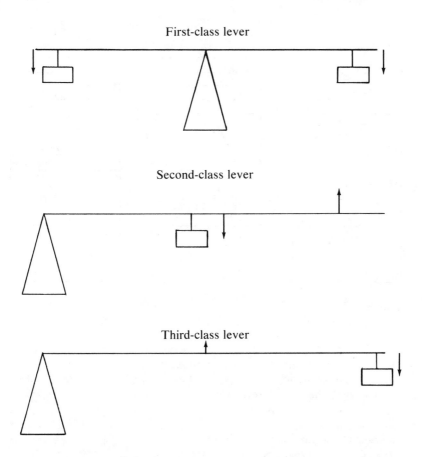

In this style, students actually "see" the meanings of the lever arrangements; they internalize the roles of the axis, resistance, and force, and in all likelihood retain it. Actually, the students do not have to memorize the details of the levers. This discovery experience provides them with the ability to reproduce this information again.

The next step in studying the levers can be applying these principles to objects, machines, etc., by Guided Discovery. Students will have no problem applying their knowledge to such traditional objects as doors, wheelbarrows, nutcrackers, and many others.

2. Focus: Systematic change   (or, learning to create a new model from a previously known one).

Setting the scene: Draw the following figures, three equal-size rectangles, divided into equal compartments.

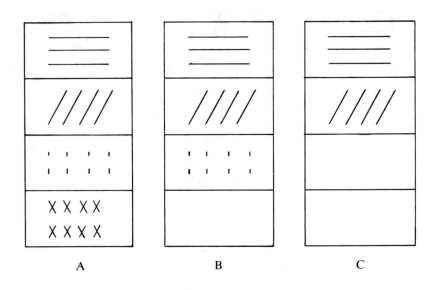

Step 1: Ask, "What is the same about A, B, and C?

Anticipated answer: "They are all boxes." ("Yes!") (Older children would say, "They are all rectangles.")

Step 2: Ask, "What else is the same?"

Anticipated answer: "They are all divided into four compartments (or four equal compartments)." ("Correct!")

Step 3: Ask, "What else is the same?"

Anticipated answer: "The (some) compartments have marks in them." ("Good!")

Step 4: Ask, "What else?"

Anticipated answer: "The top two compartments have the same markings." ("True!")

Step 5: Ask, "What's the same about A and B?"

Anticipated answer: "The top three compartments have the same markings." ("Right!")

Step 6: Ask, "Now what is the difference among A, B, and C?"

Anticipated answer: Young children say: "Each box has one thing fewer." ("Yes!") (Older children say: "Each box is different from the previous box by one thing.")

Step 7: Ask, "Could you now show what box D should look like?"

Anticipated answer:

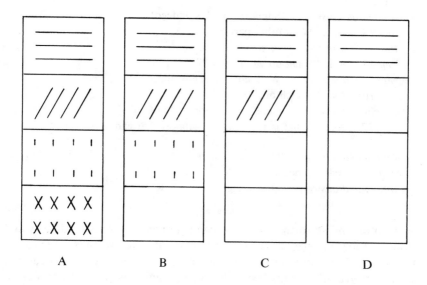

A   B   C   D

Step 8: Ask, "If we had box E, what would it look like?"
Anticipated answer: "All compartments will be empty." ("True!")

At this point we can assume that the children have internalized the principle of "keeping all variables constant except one," or the idea of systematic change. We could stop here. However, this observation of how a systematic change occurs can be quite useful, so let's continue a few more steps and see where this little exercise in observing, comparing, and contrasting can lead.

Step 9: Ask, "So, if we have a model of something and we want to make a "new" one that is different yet almost the same, what must we do?"
Anticipated answer: "Change one thing." ("Right.")
Step 10: "Say, let's see how it works with other things. Look at this chair; suppose we wanted to design another chair that looks like this one and yet will be different, what must we do?"
Anticipated answer: (At times, there will be a pause here. Now the learners have to transfer what they have previously learned.)
Step 11: "Well? What must we know first?"
Anticipated answer: "First we must know the parts of the chair."
Step 12: Say, "OK, what are the parts that all chairs must have?"
Anticipated answer: "A seat." ("Right!")

Step 13: (Someone else usually says "legs.") Say, "Not quite, instead of legs a chair must have – what? What is it that legs do – what do they give to the seat?"
Anticipated answer: "Support!" ("Yes, indeed!")
Step 14: Ask, "What other parts?"
Anticipated answer: "A back!" ("OK!")
Step 15: Ask, "What do we do now?"
Anticipated answer: "We'll change one of these."
Step 16: Ask, "Which one?"
Anticipated answer: "Let's say support." ("OK!")
Step 17: Ask, "What is the smallest support that can be designed for a chair?"
Anticipated answer: "One leg." ("Yes!")
Step 18: Ask, "What kind of a leg?"
Anticipated answer: "One straight leg." ("OK!")

And so on and so forth. Thus you can lead your students to identify and design changes in size, color, texture, materials, etc.; all these steps are a part of the focus at hand: systematic change (or you might even call it a guide for *invention*). This lesson has been taught many times to different groups across the country in demonstrations of this style. It has been interesting to observe that age levels did not really matter. (This has been tried with groups from first graders through graduate students – the same lesson, the same sequence, and practically the same language.) All age levels became involved in this game of inventing new chairs. The only noticeable difference was, at times, the *speed* of internalizing the principle and discovering or inventing new designs in a systematic way. The products have been quite the same, the direction and spirit similar.

(Comment: You might be interested to know the background of this lesson. Why would one design such a lesson? Well, over the years, working with concepts and theories of cognitive psychology and discovery processes it became clear that many students seem unable to discover or invent or "go beyond the given information." It also became clear that it was not inability but a variety of inhibitions – cognitive and emotional. Students in many classes are literally afraid to produce a response which seems to them to be different from what the teacher expects. You can also hear from teachers such statements as: "Not everyone can be creative."

Experimenting with this lesson (and many others) has shown that everyone can go beyond the given information. It is that some need to be guided more than others and some need it for a longer period of time.)

3. Focus: Discovery of a concept   The concept sought: realization of individual differences in physical ability and the design of opportunity for all in the same selected activity: the high jump.

Setting the scene: Ask the children to hold a rope which will serve as an obstacle for jumping. Invariably they will hold the rope horizontally at a given height.

Step 1: Ask the group to jump over the rope. If the rope seems too high, before the first jumper moves, ask the rope holders to lower the rope to a height which you think will provide success for all.

Step 2: Everyone jumps. After everyone clears the obstacle, you ask, "What shall we do now?" "Raise it!" is always the answer (perhaps the success by all motivates everyone to continue).

Step 3: Ask the rope holders to raise it slightly. The jumping is resumed and completed.

Step 4: "Now what?" "Raise it again," say the children.

Step 5: Raising the rope two or three more times will create a new situation: some children will not be able to clear the height. In traditional situations these children will be *eliminated* from jumping and only the "better" ones will continue; as the rope is raised there will be a constantly diminishing number of active participants. Individual differences will have been realized; the *design* for opportunity for all has not yet come about.

Step 6: Stop the jumping and ask the group: "What can we do with the rope so that nobody will be eliminated?" In short time the following answers are offered:

    a. Hold the rope higher at the two ends and let it dip at the center.

    b. Slant the rope! Hold it high at one end and low at the other.

These solutions, two alternatives of one principle, provide for continuous success for all regardless of ability level. It provides for continuous participation in the lesson which is, after all, one of the objectives of education. As far as this style of teaching is concerned, we see that in minimum steps a dilemma can be understood and alternatives offered to solve it. (This lesson, too, was taught coast to coast in the United States and Canada with strikingly similar results. Children always understood the issue and always presented these workable solutions.)

4. Focus: Examining a moral issue

Setting the scene: A child once asked me the following questions: "If a person has no home and is very hungry, is it all right for him to steal?"

Question: "Suppose I said, No, it is not all right to steal?"

Response: "Then the person will still go hungry."

Question: "How long can one go hungry?"

Response: "A few days, I guess."

Question: "And then?"

Response: "The person will die."

Question: "Is this desirable?"

Response: "No."

Question: "Then, what happens to a person who is caught stealing?"

Response: "He may be sentenced to jail?"

Question: "Is that desirable?"
Response: "Yes!"
Question: "Why?"
Response: "Because then he will be given food and shelter."
Question: "And what will that mean?"
Response: "It means that he will stay alive."
Question: "How do the two situations compare?"
Response: "Well, in this case, if you obey the law you die; if you break the law you stay alive."

The child who asked this paradoxical question was nine-and-a-half years old. The purpose of this conversation was not to establish a specific moral position but rather to identify the paradox.

Implications of Guided Discovery

Implications for Philosophy of Education

Before anyone sets out to prepare and execute lessons in Guided Discovery one must believe in the ability of students to make small discoveries and the validity of this process in guiding students along various cognitive paths. It is imperative to believe that there is value in finding out things for oneself. Then and only then will the teacher be willing to go through the time of preparing detailed, meticulous lessons and using them with utmost patience and tranquility. During demonstrations of this style one hears comments like: "Tell them the answer and get it over with," or, "Why waste time in a tedious process? You can tell them the whole thing in half the time." It is true that the teacher beginning Guided Discovery encounters many moments of frustration, particularly about time; these can be endured when one believes in the value of the process. If you believe that students should think, and think in an organized manner, then conditions must be provided for this to occur. One of these conditions is the recurrent use of Guided Discovery as a style of teaching.

Implications for Learning

This style is potent partly because it teases the curiosity of the learner. This curiosity can be maintained by appropriate sequences of questions. The very act of satisfying that curiosity, achieving consonance at every step of the way, serves as motivation to learn, motivation to start and motivation to continue. When this motivation is kindled by the series of dissonances the student becomes *actively* involved in the process. Perhaps that *is* this style's greatest asset, greatest contribution to learning. It is the kind of stimuli used by the teacher that frees the student from the state of cognitive acquiescence; it is the first style on the spectrum that deliberately *activates* specific kinds of cognitive involvement. There will be those who will argue that it is a *dangerous* style of teaching because of the precise manipulation of learning behavior. In all probability a teacher can guide a student to discover anything and this, some say, can be dangerous: brainwashing techniques are said to be similar. Perhaps one of the implications for learning is that we must be responsible in the use of Guided Discovery, particularly in areas such as social studies, political science, or any area which is sensitive to interpretative behavior. When used with the exact sciences or mathematics, learning cannot be diverted — or can it?

One more point about learning must be discussed: efficiency. The teacher uninitiated in Guided Discovery will often measure efficiency by how much time the learning experience initially requires. This, of course, is a carry-over from the Command Style where the experience is judged by the length of time it takes to *listen* to the information delivered; learning is assessed by the amount *remembered* as a result of listening.

Now, Guided Discovery takes longer than previous styles if we measure learning only by the *amount* of subject matter covered. However, if learning is more than just listening and remembering, then time has new meaning. Since Guided Discovery invokes a variety of different cognitive operations not invoked by other styles, time must be allotted for these to occur. Moreover, as proficiency in this teaching style develops, less time is required to reach any given goal. In addition, some of the cognitive activities upheld as virtues of the Command Style, specifically memory, are enhanced by participating in discovery. Researchers in this area have suggested that when you discover something you will remember more of it, and for a longer time (Katona, 29; Bruner, 12). And then there is the student's excitement to consider, that emotional awareness that one has discovered for oneself — even though perhaps it was only a small bit of information.

**Implications for Status on
the Developmental
Channels**

It is difficult to hypothesize about the relationship between Guided Discovery and the position on the physical developmental channel. Further studies in this area are necessary. It is equally difficult to make

Theoretical Limits Concept

Command Style	Task Style	Reciprocal Style	Individual Program	Guided Discovery	?
Minimum ←				→ Maximum	
				?	
Physical development				X	
			?		
Social development			X		
Emotional development					X
Intellectual development					X

a definitive statement concerning the social developmental channel. The small discoveries, those moments of attaining insight at a given step of the process are the property of the responding individual. These discoveries do not belong to the group, although the process can be a group one. A group cannot discover, an individual can. But perhaps the cumulative effect of discoveries by group members can create a sense of participating in a common discovery project. It is difficult to prove that this kind of participation is a socializing process since the interaction among the members of the group is kept to a minimum. The transaction actually occurs between the teacher (as a central figure who emits the stimuli) and each individual in the group who wishes to offer an overt response.

Though when a group Guided Discovery session is executed smoothly it *looks* like a group effort, behaviorally it is not. The *decisions* to respond and about the kind of response (the content) are always the individual's. What actually happens is that various individuals *randomly* participate in *adding* information by responding to the teacher's sequential stimuli — questions or clues. The others listen and accept or reject the response offered, or do not even listen. During an alert, dynamic session the third possibility may be greatly reduced but the first two still exist. In a group there is *always* someone who discovers the answer *first* and proclaims it first; we can only assume that other members of the class also discovered while still others listened to the first response. These, then, have not participated in the act of discovery to its fullest. Some were subjected to the stimulus, perhaps engulfed by the state of cognitive dissonance, but never reached fruition. They neither discovered nor offered an overt response. This is one of the drawbacks of using this style with a group. With very small groups the chances to elicit more frequent responses from each member increase, but even in a small group there is always a first responder to each question in the sequence. Nevertheless, the major assets of Guided Discovery are its ability to in-

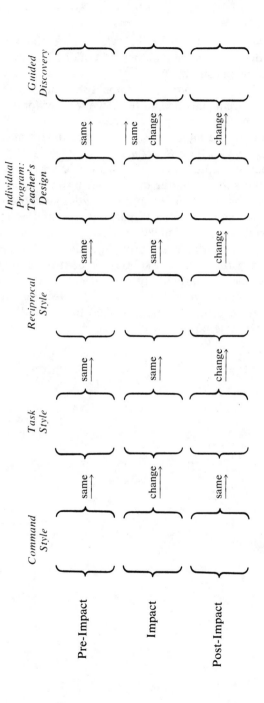

voke a *particular cognitive operation.* No other style so far on the spectrum has had this capability.

Before we move on to the next style let's identify once more the specific shift in decisions in the Anatomy of Guided Discovery that occurred (see the diagram on page 143):

Besides the change in the post-impact set where evaluation and feedback decisions are made once more by the teacher (or the teaching agent: the teaching machine, the programmed materials, etc.), the *significant change* occurs at the impact set, where the student makes, for the first time, decisions about the *subject matter.*

Each decision represented in an *answer* or any other overt response constitutes the subject matter discovered by the student. Though it is true that this subject matter is congruent with that chosen by the teacher, it *is* a decision about the subject matter discovered by the student. One of the powerful aspects of Guided Discovery is this bond between student and subject matter, an intimacy brought about by this cognitive flow.

We can say that this is a subtle — or controlled — shift in decisions about subject matter, particularly since it occurs during the impact set. It must not be confused with subject matter decisions made during the pre-impact set. Will these ever be shifted to the student? Is it the next step? The next style on the Spectrum?

8 Problem Solving

The next step on the spectrum of teaching styles is the next level of discovery: Problem Solving. The essential difference between Guided Discovery and Problem Solving is in the *deployment* of the cognitive powers. Guided Discovery uses convergent thinking, which means that the student makes only certain, limited decisions about the subject matter, limited in order to be congruent with decisions previously made by the teacher. Problem Solving uses *divergent thinking,* which means that the student can make any decision about the subject matter as long as the problem at hand is solved. This style of teaching appears here on the spectrum because it provides for *more* student decision making, more in both quantity and quality. It provides for decisions about *alternatives* in solutions, one of the most striking consequences of Problem Solving.

Cognition is a process that unleashes the mind, releases inhibitions to think in a given path; it calls for another solution, it seeks the different, it uncovers the unknown. Yet, cognition is not quite completely in its finest bloom because in this style decisions about the *problems themselves* are still made by the teacher.

Though the student is invited to participate not only in the act of solving but in the discovery of alternative solutions, making decisions about the kind of responses, the teacher still chooses the problems to be solved.

Problem Solving as it appears on the spectrum projects a high level of the individualizing process which began with the shift from the Command to the Task Style and which elicits man's ability to conceive and produce new solutions, information, and knowledge. Theoretically, any given problem that faces the learner has the potential to stimulate the production of one or more solutions, which are the consequences of one or more cognitive operations. The problem creates cognitive dissonance, which evokes inquiry, stimulating specific cognitive activities which result in a definite product — a solution or *solutions.* Again, it is necessary to emphasize that the uniqueness of this style is not the inquiry processes (also intrinsic to Guided Discovery) but rather the *results* of these processes — *the production of alternatives*. Most if not all problems have more than one solution. This teaching style not only encourages production of multiple solutions but provides conditions for this to occur; schematically:

A problem → cognitive dissonance → inquiry → solutions

The problem, the initial stimulus, is followed by the mediation period (we saw the S–M–R in Guided Discovery) in which one or more specific cognitive operations act to produce their solutions. The relationships among the stimuli, the mediation activity, and the ensuing responses can be represented thus:

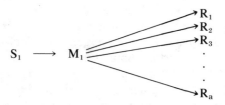

A particular problem (S_1) is dealt with and possibly solved by a particular mediation activity (M_1 can be any one of the cognitive operations). This particular mediation activity can produce one or more solutions (R_1; R_2; R_3; . . . R_a), which may be *known*, to some people, or *unknown*. In either case the sum of these responses, the sum of these solutions constitutes cumulative information, knowledge about the problem. It constitutes *subject matter* evolved through discovery by the student.

Now, when presented with the next problem the process is expressed:

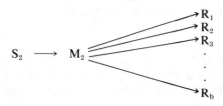

The next particular problem (S_2) may be dealt with via the same or another set of mediation activities (M_2) which produce another array of solutions (R_1; R_2; R_3; . . . ; R_b).

These solutions, too, constitute subject matter, information, knowledge. Thus we can see that a *series* of problems can bring about a variety of bits of information, an accumulation of subject matter. The most striking feature of this process is that it is *open ended*. Theoretically, it is an infinite process; theoretically, an infinite number of problems can be identified or designed in any issue, in any subject. These problems, in turn, will keep producing new realizations, new insights, new solutions, new ideas, new knowledge. All done by individual students who have learned to make decisions *independent* of the teachers' preconceived solutions and decisions.

All previous styles dealt with *past knowledge;* Problem Solving deals with the *past and future knowledge.* Allowing students to solve problems means participation in the mystery, excitement, fear, and joy of evolving new ideas, of joining the most dynamic human process of them all—becoming.

Now, on the operational, or practical, level, this process can be examined from three different points of view: *the possible, the feasible,* and *the desirable.*

a. the possible   This level of solutions to problems contains and accepts *any* solution that *solves the given problem.* Its rationale is intellectual freedom to produce limitlessly. This level is devoid of any value system; it is not concerned with "right" or "wrong," "good" or "bad," useful or not. It is only concerned with the flow of solutions that solve the problem.

Let's not be alarmed, though: we aren't discussing implementation of these possible solutions, but merely the fact that there are different ways of treating the products of cognition. It is imperative to alert teachers to the different level of solutions. Too many teachers, in too many areas of study, curtail and deliberately diminish the cognitive flow of children by pre-selecting solutions by personal biases and preferences. Children learn early in school to produce the answer the teacher wishes to hear. The flow of solutions is *intrinsic* to the particular cognitive process of seeking answers, seeking alternatives. Let's examine some examples:

In arithmetic, if the problem is to find ways of producing the number five by addition, subtraction, and division, the number of *possible* and correct solutions is infinite. Even if the problem is delimited by establishing 100 as the largest number to be used in this problem, the number of solutions is huge. The act of solving this problem *calls* for all *possible* solutions. It is not concerned with preferences by any criteria, only the possible.

In social studies, if the problem presented to students is the issue of identifying the conflicts of a minority in a society, and developing plans to solve these conflicts, students who are accustomed to think freely will produce an incredible number of solutions which will cover the gamut from total assimilation to annihilation. All these solutions are *possible;* they are the products of discovering and inventing value-free solutions. (Certainly, each solution can, and perhaps *must,* be followed through, analyzed, and made to yield conclusions about its contributions and hazards for a given society. This, however, is another, a subsequent problem in the issue at hand.)

As another example, suppose you could alter human anatomy by adding an arm to the human body, where would you attach it, and why? Obviously, the possibilities are infinite; however, it is most fascinating and amusing to hear students' solutions and observe the reactions of others when you play this game with different classes.

One of the commonest reactions when you ask your students to announce their solutions one after the other is to play it safe. Many will say, "My solution is like his." Apparently there are inhibitions against reaching for all possibilities, at least when asked for a public response.

Seeking all possibilities can be done in every area of learning and action—the sciences, the arts, social studies, human movement, music, mathematics, drama, literature, etc. If a teacher wants students to recruit, develop, and fathom their abilities to solve problems it must be done freely, without boundaries and without moralizing. When one operates on the level of the *possible,* all solutions are acceptable.

b. the feasible   This level of solutions to problems contains and accepts *only* solutions that *seem* to be feasible. Feasibility is determined by a set of criteria that delineates the *conditions* for feasibility, which includes:

1. Economics. It may be *possible* to build a particular bridge, but the decision to do so will depend on whether or not it is economically *feasible.*

2. Efficiency. There are many *possible* mechanical inventions. Which solution to use depends on the efficiency of the suggested machine; certain efficiencies are feasible, others are not.

3. Time. In some cases, solutions which take less time to execute are more feasible than those requiring more time, regardless of *other* beneficial qualities. This example will apply in test situations where students are evaluated by the number of correct solutions they can offer in a prescribed length of time.

4. Others? Can you suggest categories of criteria by which feasibility must sometimes be determined?

We could conclude that feasibility criteria are used as selective measures to *decide* which solutions to accept and which to reject. We could say, then, that *possible* solutions are always more numerous than *feasible* solutions.

c. the desirable   This level of solutions to problems contains and accepts *only* solutions that *are said to be right*. The desirability is determined by cultural criteria or personal beliefs (morality, legality, beauty, etc.). Decisions about right and wrong are always rooted in cultural determinants. These sets of criteria will include:

1. Political beliefs. It may be possible to behave in a particular way, it may even be feasible—but it is *not desirable*. Desirability reflects the political beliefs which establish the limits by which other people are forced to live. A most vivid example of condemning people's solutions is the announcement of the names of sixty-five people declared to be "undesirable" by the standards of the House Internal Security Committee (see New York Times, October 15, 1970), compiled from lists of college campus speakers who offered alternative solutions to problems that plague our civilization and humanity: war, destruction, hunger, oppression, and so on.

   Suppose this issue is raised in your class—or better yet, suppose *you* raised the issue and the problem in your class (of course, it is *possible* that by doing so you may risk adding your name to the list), how would you handle the possible solutions offered by members of the class? How would you handle solutions which *are* or *are not* desirable by the criterion of political acceptability?

2. Aesthetics. These include all the decisions about what *looks* attractive or not and, therefore, desirable or not. Examples of what these codes mean to school life are superfluous in this context. Suffice it to mention the behavior of principals, faculties, coaches, and others who impose, or attempt to impose, their aesthetic standards on students.

3. Morality. Designed to select desirable from undesirable behavior in matters of friendship, loyalty, love, sex, interpretation of social events, and so on.

4. Rules of a transaction, a situation, a game. These are designed to sift the "feasible" from the "possible" and select only the "desirable" to comply with the rules which presently prevail, such as in behavior in traffic, in religious conduct, in industry, in sports, and in many other areas.

5. Other?

We can conclude that the number of desirable solutions many times (not always) is less than the number of feasible solutions. The use of value judgment always curtails the number of desirable solutions.

While other styles of teaching represent the process of *cognitive reduction,* Problem Solving stimulates *cognitive expansion*. It seems that all previous teaching styles on the spectrum deal with "the desirable" as determined by teachers (with their own personal biases and value systems), curriculum committees, boards of education. At times these styles offer and handle "the feasible," as long as it does not disturb the equilibrium established by "the desirable."

Before we move on, would you like to participate in a short problem-solving session? Could you identify in your teaching, if you have used Problem Solving, situations when you accepted and treated objectively *all* possible solutions offered by your students? Did your acceptance reinforce your students and motivate them to offer more, or did it hinder them?

Can you identify situations when you rejected solutions because they were not feasible? How did you explain this to your class? Did you offer criteria? Did they accept your criteria? Did they themselves examine their solutions against your criteria, or did you do it for them? Were they encouraged by your behavior (your decisions) to offer more solutions to the problems at hand? Did they readily participate in subsequent sessions? Did you wait?

Can you identify situations when you engaged in congnitve reduction by rejecting your students' solutions because they were not desirable? What did you tell them? Did you offer criteria for rejection? Were these personal criteria, indigenous to a segment of the population? Did you tell them that? Did your student belong to that segment? Were there any "outsiders" in the class? Did the "insiders" accept the criteria for desirability? Did the "outsiders" accept? Did anyone challenge the criteria? (If not—why not?) Did anyone offer alternative criteria? How did you handle the alternative proposal?

After answering these questions to your satisfaction would you say that your behavior was conducive to the process of Problem Solving and cognitive expansion?

Anatomy of Teaching by Problem Solving

Pre-Impact Set
Who makes what decisions

Decision categories	The teacher	The student
Geography	Ascertains availability of space for individual work. (Some problems in some fields require doing some work in other parts of the school building. This needs to be prepared in advance.)	Not involved.
Time	People vary, often radically, in the amount of time needed for solving problems of comparable difficulty; this necessitates provision for time flexibility.	Not involved.

This highly *individualized* use of time is alien to a teacher accustomed to making time decisions for a group where the "average" (a most repulsive idea to cognitive development) students are always the determinant of pace.

(Also, though it is difficult, it is necessary for the novice to move about, observe and *not talk*. Excellent sources to study this issue are the works on "Interaction Analysis" by Flanders (17) and Amidon (3).)

A decision about the "free time" that is suddenly available to the teacher must be made. This time can be used for intense, continuous observation of individual students, to learn how your students perceive problems and go about solving them; how they offer solutions and how they examine their solutions. It is a time for intimacy between student and subject matter, and for delicate, direct relationships between teacher and student. A decision has to be made now (and rechecked during the impact set) about whether or not the teacher should interfere in the student's intimacy at any given point.

This time can be used to offer help to those who need it or ask for it. Decisions must be made now (and rechecked during the impact set) about the kind of difficulties that might arise during the process.

While involved with an individual student, the teacher may sometimes tend to solve the problem for the student. This must be avoided by a pre-impact decision (to be rechecked and adjusted during the impact set) concerning the anticipated obstacles involved in the given subject matter.

Quantity and quality	These decisions cannot be made by the teacher, but are made by the student in the impact set.	Not involved.
Organization	Mainly about the use of equipment. A different kind of equipment distribution and availability will be needed to depend on the pace of each student. More (and sometimes all) pieces of equipment may be used at the same time. Some teachers need to adjust to this.	Not involved.
Subject matter	Probably most difficult and most crucial in preparation for problem solving sessions, creating the appropriate problems for a class requires an understanding of problem design and the relationship between problems and the structure of subject matter — not only knowledge of some facts but of their interrelation-ships.	Not involved.
Communica-tion mode	The *techniques* of presenting the problems, such as orally (which presents memory prob-lems for some students), or written, or etc.	Not involved.

Impact Set
Who makes what decisions

Decision categories	The teacher	The student
Geography	Not involved.	By now the students know how to handle space, and know where they wish to be while solving problems.
Time	Not involved.	Students are totally free to make time decisions, particu-larly duration. They are the only ones who know how long they need to solve a problem.

Quantity and quality	Not involved. Quality decisions may be made and conveyed later, after the student is comfortable in the process and the criteria for quality are understood.	Quantity decisions are made by students based on their individual ability to use time for this purpose. Quality decisions are intrinsic to the very act of solving. The students are making subject matter decisions – the solutions they choose to use and present are the reflection of *their* decisions about quality.
Organization	Not involved.	Performs all.
Subject matter	Involved only in the design of the problems.	Involved in seeking and verifying solutions – a personal process: Each student enters the process in a different way, in a different pace, with different intensity and intent, etc.
Adjustment	Necessary when a teacher observes retreat behavior. A student may not have understood the problem(s) (reiteration may suffice), or may not see the relevance of the problem(s) to the issue at hand (an explanation might work), or may not understand a word, a term, a phrase.	Not involved.

Post-Impact Set
Who makes what decisions

Decision categories	The teacher	The student
All decisions	In this style both the teacher and student are involved in post-impact decisions, though each in a different way. There are several *kinds* of post-impact decisions made by the teacher: a. Silent decisions about the student's solutions, *while* the student is engaged in impact decisions: Most common in subjects which require from the student an	Post-impact decisions involve immediate feedback and evaluation of results. Both activities are inherent in the act of solving. In most cases (it varies with the subject matter) the student *knows* whether or not the problem has been solved and often he also knows the correctness, the value of the solution, and when the problem *is not* solved. (In this case the

immediate overt response such as in music, human movement, chemistry experiment, shop, etc.

b. Delayed decisions. These occur when time has elapsed between the student's impact decisions and the teacher's seeing them, as in reading written solutions, checking a model which represents the solution(s), evaluating a chart, diagram, etc.

c. Validity decisions: evaluation of the problems themselves, to ascertain that as designed they bring about solutions relevant to the subject matter. If inappropriate they should be deleted.

d. Feedback and termination decisions, about the *kind* and *frequency* of feedback to be delivered to the student. These will differ from student to student, but they must be made in order to achieve a conclusion, the student's sense of completion.

student makes a decision about a choice among three possibilities: (a) tackle the problem again, (b) retreat, (c) seek aid.) By the self-feedback the student can make a decision about the next step.

The student may make decisions to request information about his performance. The assumption here is that despite the longevity of involvement that occurs to students learning by problem solving, most students need periodical conclusion (some need it less frequently). They need to know from outside sources that their solutions are accepted, good, important, and relevant.

Problem Solving, the Structure of Subject Matter, and Cognitive Operations

Several interesting and puzzling aspects of Problem Solving as a teaching style confront the teacher. First is the relationship between problems and the structure of the subject matter. The fact that one can design problems in a given subject and produce a variety of appropriate solutions elicits a variety of necessary questions: "Do we design just *any* problem that comes to mind? Do we ask any question that seems relevant to the subject matter?" "Do we do it in any arbitrary fashion?" "Should there be any order in problem design?" "What are the advantages and disadvantages in each approach?"

Arbitrary problems presented to a class can bring about responses within the context of the subject matter. One can present a class with valid problems that may be interesting for some, are relevant to the respective disciplines, and will result in solutions—most likely variable solutions—and will employ some kind of cognitive activity, *but:*

a. Are these the *first* questions one asks in the given subject?
b. If they are, then why? What is the rationale?
c. If they are not, then which questions should precede?
d. What are the *next* questions?
e. Must there be order?
f. Since problem solving is an open-ended process of divergent thinking, can we design open-ended problems, which will always leave room for further problems, further questions?

One way to resolve this series of questions is by identifying a relationship between problem design and the structure of subject matter. Structure of subject matter is rather complex; it involves inquiry into what makes a discipline what it is—that is, it involves insights into the structure of knowledge, theory of knowledge, and proposals of what it is and what it can become. (See Bruner (10, 11) and Broudy, Smith, and Burnett (8).)

Equally complex and important are (*a*) the relationship between problem-solving behavior and the structure of subject matter, and (*b*) the relationship that *exists* or *may exist* between a *particular* cognitive operation and the *different* aspects of the subject matter. For example, let us assume that any subject matter is composed of facts, concepts, etc. To find out whether a student has learned "the facts" of the subject matter we can use *questions geared for recall;* the cognitive operation elicited is *memory.* On the other hand, if we wish the student to "see" the concept that binds seemingly scattered facts, a different cognitive operation will have to be induced: *compare and contrast and draw conclusions.* It is clear, then, that *conceptually* and *linguistically* the question (the problem) must be different. One kind of questioning will elicit memory, another comparing and contrasting.

Another major problem concerns the relationship between the two problems, *a* and *b,* and the "kind" of discipline in which we design problems. Physics, mathematics, chemistry, etc., are not the same *kind* of disciplines as history, political science, sociology, cultural anthropology, etc.: the first cluster can be called the "hard" disciplines; the second cluster, the "soft" disciplines. The hard disciplines can be considered universal, that is, transcultural, disciplines while the soft disciplines are more indigenous to a particular culture or dependent upon interpretation by individuals or subculture groups in the application of evaluative principles to data. Awareness of this distinction and of its relationship to teaching styles, particularly Problem Solving, is particularly relevant to solutions to social issues in which one's value system is the major determinant not only in selection among available solutions but also in the creation of the solutions themselves (see the section on the possible, feasible, desirable levels of Solutions, pp. 147–149).

Below is a model of the relationships among these problems:

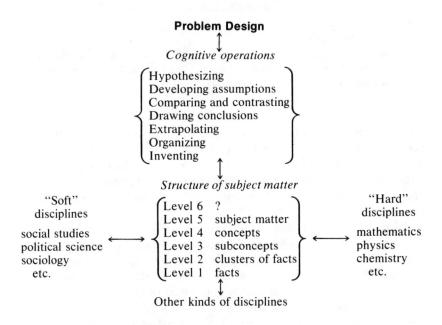

The model suggests reciprocal relationships among a discipline, a level in the structure of its subject matter, a cognitive operation or set of operations, and the design of a problem or set of problems. Read from top to bottom, it suggests that in any discipline a problem or set of problems can be designed which will deliberately invoke a particular cognitive operation that will elicit responses (solutions) at one level of the structure of its subject matter; *specifically* (and only as an example), this model poses the following *steps* in the following problem: How do you (1) *design a problem* that will (2) *invoke the act* of developing assumptions about (3) *specific subconcepts* which are a part of subject matter in cultural geography representing knowledge in (4) *one of the other social sciences?*

In order to solve the posed problem one must know the disciplines, be competent in their subject matter, understand their structure, and be familiar with cognitive activities. Then and only then can one design problems relevant to the discipline, the solutions of which will be congruent with present knowledge in the discipline.

Any discipline contains a huge number of "bits of information," ideas, concepts, relationships and it also possesses *potential* bits of information, ideas, concepts, etc., that will be discovered, created, or invented as knowledge constantly increases in every area. This condition of expansion and mobility of human knowledge and experience has raised some critical questions for educators:

1. What should be taught?
2. How do we select from this enormous amount of available information?
3. How do we know what is of primary importance and what is of secondary and tertiary importance in any given area of subject matter?
4. How do we distinguish between assembly of information and acquisition of knowledge?
5. How do we teach for *further* assembly of information (information yet to be revealed) and further acquisition of knowledge (knowledge yet to be discovered)?
6. How do we handle the dilemma of "fixed" knowledge and "flux" in knowledge?
7. How do we teach students to learn the limits of their knowledge – that is, to become aware of what they know and of what they do not know?
8. How do we (or can we) resolve those issues by using Problem Solving as a teaching style?

The Structure of Subject Matter

Understanding the structure of subject matter may give us insights into what makes a given subject *what it is* and yet keep it open and flexible to provide for *what it might become.* The model for the *structure of subject matter,* below, is arranged by *levels* because there is a hierarchy in the structure of any subject matter, reflected in the complexity of both the *content* at a given level and the *cognitive processes* involved at that level.

"Moving up" the hierarchy of the structure of subject matter depends on the *relationships* that exist or may exist between any two levels. These relationships must first be perceived and understood, and then and only then one can see or apply the entire structure, or its parts, for a chosen purpose. (Examples will follow!)

Level 1, the facts   are the present scattered "bits of information," the truths, the smallest parts of the given subject matter (real or imaginary): the array of numbers in arithmetic; single events, names, dates, etc., in history; the myriad sounds in music; in human movement (dance, gymnastics, ball games, etc.), any jump, step, purposive movement, etc.

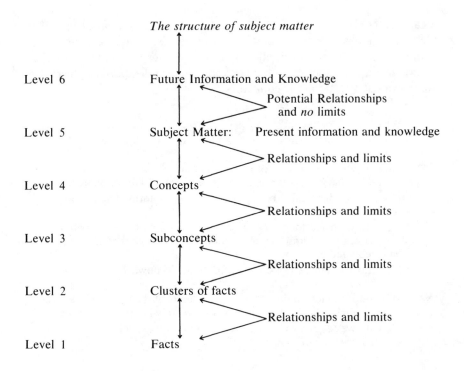

The structure of subject matter

But an accumulation of the facts in any subject is no more than just a pile of facts until something is done with them. (The futile controversies about *knowledge of facts* versus *understanding* which flares up from time to time has *absolutely* no place here. Understanding of the relationship between the structure of subject matter and cognitive operations may make such discussions less likely.) Since facts, as defined here, are the smallest units of the structure of subject matter, they seem fixed, unalterable—at least for a certain length of time. In some subjects, facts seem permanently fixed—for example, in history certain events, considered independently of any interpretation, are immutable facts, as are certain events in physics, or as are the letters or characters of any alphabet. For teaching or learning facts, the most prevalent cognitive operation is *memory*. One either remembers the facts of a subject or does not; rarely is there a need for other (certainly not many other) operations for the facts alone. (Can you identify in your field of teaching the facts of your subject matter? Are they now the same as you thought they were before? Are they different? Why? Do you have a different definition and conception of facts?)

Level 2, the clusters of facts   contain the first grouping of facts. If two or more facts can be grouped by *any* criterion (any principle, any idea, any thread of similarity), they are a cluster. There are good examples in history. This is a problem for you to solve: What are some facts in any branch of history that can be grouped together by some criterion to form a cluster?

What about several sounds produced by the *same* musical instrument in the key of A major? Two factors connect the scattered individual sounds: the same key and the same instrument. One common factor suffices for the creation of a cluster.

The "sets" in mathematics are an example of clusters.

Suppose you saw a dance with a series of jumps and leaps – all different, each one a separate movement instance. How would you connect these facts into a cluster?

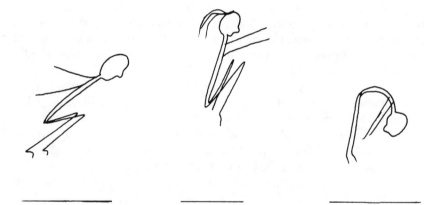

These three separate jumps are members of a cluster because they all represent the idea of "off the ground."

In language, the letters of an alphabet are grouped together to form a cluster – a word. The connecting factor is the meaning attached to that group of letters which form a given word in a given language. Of course, this connecting factor is culturally determined, while the leaps, connected by a physical factor, are universal.

Two or more bricks cemented together form a cluster. They are on the way to becoming something other than just a pile of bricks.

The *major* aspect that differentiates a cluster of facts from level one is the realization and identification of *a relationship* among the scattered facts. This realization *intrinsically requires* the employment of cognitive operations *other* than memory. You cannot, in any field, conceive, recognize, or construct a cluster without at least the following cognitive operations:

a. compare and contrast
b. analyze
c. draw conclusions (identifying relationships)
d. arrange and organize

(Can you identify in your field of teaching the clusters in your subject matter? Are they, now, the same as you thought they were before? Are they different? Why?)

Level 3, the subconcepts   contain the grouping of similar *clusters*. If two or more clusters have, by any criterion, a common factor, they can be grouped together to form a *subconcept*. The number set with the subscript identifying the base is an example of grouping clusters into a subconcept. Combining words into a sentence is grouping clusters into a subconcept. A musical phrase is a subconcept composed of clusters of connected sounds. Clusters of leaps and jumps are grouped together to represent the subconcept of agility. Several clusters of bricks cemented together can form a wall, which is a subconcept. (Can you offer similar examples in your field?)

Again, moving up to this level requires several cognitive activities. (As a matter of fact, right now as you read you are probably engaged in trying to figure out one of two things, or both: (*a*) Are these proposals possible, feasible, sensible, logically consistent? (*b*) Do they apply to my field? To answer these questions you *must* engage in the proposed cognitive operations — indeed, you cannot escape it!)

Engaging in level three, identifying subconcepts in a given field elicits the following cognitive activities at least:

1. To group clusters into a subconcept:

a. comparing and contrasting
b. analyzing
c. drawing conclusions
d. arranging and organizing
e. reexamining for consistency
f. others?

2. To state the subconcept:

a. identifying similarities (an idea, principle, law, etc.)
b. understanding ("seeing") the kind of *relationships*
c. structuring the subconcept
d. checking its validity
e. making linguistic decisions about how to state the subconcept.
f. others?

It was previously suggested that the structure of subject matter is a hierarchy of complexity in both content and cognitive involvement. Can you accept this assertion? Is it now true that level three is richer and more complex in content than levels two and one? And is it not true that level three requires more numerous cognitive operations, which are perhaps also more complex and demand more than, say, memory alone?

Level 4, concepts   group subconcepts with some common aspect into an encompassing concept. In mathematics several subconcepts may join together to represent the concepts of "more than," "less than," "equal," "not equal," "true," "not true," etc. In social studies, there are such concepts of human events or needs as: "settling," "revolution," "shelter," "war," etc. In music the concerto, symphony, etc., are concepts. In human movement, "transporting the body," "the body in repose," etc., are concepts.

The essence of the concept level is *universality,* all-inclusiveness within the given discipline — at least within the present state of knowledge — assembly of much information and an acquisition of wide knowledge are both needed, in order to embrace the conceptual level, in both content and cognitive participation.

Level 5, the subject matter   contains the categorized grouping of *all presently known* concepts in a particular field: its bodies of information and of knowledge, highly and meticulously arranged so that all data have a place, and each fact, cluster, subconcept, and concept a relationship to its antecedent and consequence.

Level 6, future information and knowledge   "contain" the yet unknown. Moving up among previous levels was done by identifying the limits of each level and the relationships between any two levels. This level, the unknown, keeps the structure of subject matter *open ended!* It provides for the *mobility* and *flexibility* in human knowledge, for future conception, realization, imagery, discovery, and invention. It provides for those cognitive operations that burst present boundaries, for the imagination of man that defies any inhibition.

These six integrated levels point to the *structure of subject matter, present and future.*

Problem Design for Specific
Levels in the Structure

Perhaps it is clearer now that a cohesive set of problems for students must be designed to be relevant and related to a *specific* level of the structure, and to invoke the particular cognitive activity (or activities) most appropriate to that level. Though quite a task, it is necessary if a teacher has a commitment to the integrity of learning, teaching, and knowledge. Let's examine some examples. Human movement is highly visible and can be readily scrutinized. Suppose we set out to design problems in *vaulting*. A person is confronted with a physical obstacle usually called a Swedish box, a vaulting box, or a horse. Our task is to investigate, by means of Problem Solving, the various possible ways for a person to vault over the obstacle.

Now, there are clearly a variety of vaults that some students and the teacher will already have done. Performing these will constitute *recall,* activation of memory, which, of course, is neither problem-solving behavior nor divergent thinking; this behavior is level one on the structure.

Some of the subconcepts (level 3) in vaulting include:

a.   direction of the vault
b.   postural variability in flight over the obstacle
c.   others?

So, let us design problems that will elicit responses (solutions) which will focus on manipulation of direction. Setting the scene will include requesting the student to vault a few times over the obstacle *without* any specified instructions, which will result in an arbitrary array of vaults, some similar (novices usually feel secure by copying) and some will be varied in different ways. (Your role is to accept all the vaults; this can be done without fanfare; merely nod your head, say "yes," and generally avoid projecting rejection of any response.)

Ask: "What are the similarities among all the vaults we have just seen?" Verbal responses will be forthcoming (wait for the responses! Don't jump the gun!). They will include statements like: All cleared the obstacle; all the vaulters touched the obstacle in some way; in all vaults the body assumed a particular posture, etc.

Ask: "What are some of the differences among these vaults?" The responses might refer to variations in posture, height of the vault, speed of approach run and vault, direction of the approach run and the direction of the body while in flight, and so on. Focus the experience by asking: "How was the direction varied?" The responses will include: forward, sideways, in various angles, etc. Acknowledge the responses and continue, "Here are some questions about the factor of direction":

1.   How do you change the direction of the vault? What are some of the things involved in this change?
2.   How much change can occur in the direction?
3.   Is there a minimum? What is it?
4.   Is there a maximum? What is it?

5. Select one of the directions, stay with it for awhile. Does it provide for more than one vault?
6. Does it provide for several? Many? Indefinite? (Ask your students to try their solutions in action whenever possible.)
7. Is there an easy, easier, or easiest direction?
8. What differentiates the difficulty among the directions?
9. What limitations are imposed on the vaulter when the direction becomes harder?
10. Which vaults (from number 6) cannot be performed as the direction becomes harder?
11. Which direction provides for the least possible number of vaults? Why?
12. Which direction provides for the largest possible number of vaults? Why?
13. Are direction and speed at all related? Does the speed of approach and flight vary with change in direction? How?
14. Which direction(s) provides for maximum speed?
15. Do all directions provide for minimum speed?
16. Is there a direction that cannot be used for vaulting? Why?
17. Is it possible to combine directions?
18. What are some ways to combine directions?
19. Do these combinations facilitate some of the vaults? Which?
20. Do some combinations (which?) inhibit some of the vaults? Which?

—and so on. Clearly the answers, cognitively conceived and physically verified or denied, are part of the subject of vaulting, information and knowledge. All these problems were directed at the subconcept of *direction* in vaulting. Can you identify which cognitive operations were activated? Many more problems can be designed for this subconcept. The second subconcept in vaulting mentioned above is postural variability in flight. Try to develop a series of problems for this subconcept. How would you start? How would you focus the students' thinking and performing on postural variability? What would be your first question?

(In classes where vaulting was taught by Problem Solving the students learned, cognitively and physically, an incredible number of vaults, most of which are not in any of the traditional gymnastics books. They learned not only to perform well but also to design the vaults and understand the various principles involved. Perhaps the most important facet of these months-long experiences is that their vaulting repertoire never ran dry; there was always a new vault to perform—a fact that kept the psychological motivation and the physical challenge high.)

Have you noticed that *none* of the questions are directed at evoking recall? Nor is *this* question to *you* a question which you can answer by recall; you'll have to reread the questions, *think* about their meaning and *analyze* the possibilities they provoke! All of these questions can be answered by engaging in a variety of cognitive activities *other than* memory. All are questions (problems) *relevant* to the structure of the subject matter. Now, if a person is interested in vaulting at all, each of these problems can create a cognitive dissonance which leads to inquiry and eventually to solution or solutions. The problems, then, are relevant to the learner.

Problem Solving means cognitive activity *other* than memory. (When you remember a solution, you remember a response which is not yours; when you solve a problem, the response is yours.) Also, most, if not all, of the questions allow *more than one answer*. This, of course, complies with the theory and psychology of Problem Solving. Furthermore, to solve the proposed problems one must examine solutions for their possibility, feasibility, and desirability. Involvement in learning seems to be total, open, free.

Let's try a similar problem design in social studies. Suppose we examine the issue of "revolution" — a marvelous topic for Problem Solving (provided the teacher is not hung up in preconceived notions about revolution), because is it not true that in many social studies classes all over the country major issues are rarely examined? Is it not true that teachers impose their own — almost always "orthodox" — values on such events rather than develop the students' ability to inquire, to see different sides, to examine evidence — varied evidence — and then draw conclusions?

We are using the Problem Solving Style to teach the student the *concept* of revolution to enable him to draw conclusions based on knowledgeable analysis and some degree of objectivity and intellectual honesty. The student should then be able to treat any revolution in this manner. (We *are* discussing the teaching and learning of the concept of a revolution, not the emotions of being involved in one.)

Here are some questions (problems) that can start and perhaps stir an open process of inquiry into this issue: What is a revolution? What is the meaning of the word? (We don't want its dictionary definition, which would limit discussion of the word. Nor are we looking for *recall*. If it moves in this direction, immediately inject an adjustment decision and rephrase the question: "What does the word revolution mean to you?" This will insure *diversity* of responses — proper problem solving behavior. In fact, this process is most fascinating with naive students such as fourth and fifth grade elementary school children: they *produce* very interesting ideas once they finish spouting the things they have been told about it. In order to insure the conditions for diversity of statements about the topic, particularly one this sensitive, the teacher must be *accepting* of *all* responses — absolutely *no* moralizing or criticizing. A teacher who has done excessive moralizing and criticizing about other topics or daily classroom occurrences *may* fail to create the proper climate for dealing with this topic. Students, who are generally quite astute, sensitive, and self-protective, will not participate unless they feel safe.)

Once one definition (if the class has agreed on one) or several defini-
tions have been offered you are ready to move to the next question. (By
the way, which cognitive operation(s) did the first question activate?)
Ask: "Why does man revolt?" Reasons will flood in. (Remember, we are
investigating for *all possible* reasons—no selected or *desirable* ones
based on *your* political orientation, social restrictions or emotional inhibition—all the reasons for every kind of revolution—political, social,
educational, sexual, artistic, aesthetic, religious, and so on.) List them all
on the blackboard. Ask for more, and wait for the responses. *Never rush
a problem solver!* This is more trying for the teacher who thinks all possibilities on a given question have been exhausted. This is the time to
wait some more! (Of course, there are alternatives. You could ask your
students if they need more time; they will tell you. Or use a group of
cards with problems written on them so that the *solving process* can be
done by pairs, small groups, or individually. These are pedagogical-
organizational decisions that must be individually made. There may be
other *procedural* alternatives.)

The "first inning" of random responses to the question why man
revolts can be grouped into categories such as: (a) political reasons, (b)
economic reasons, (c) social reasons, (d) personal, emotional reasons,
(e) ethnic or nationalistic reasons, (f) historical reasons, (g) many others
—would you name some?

Invariably, the responses fall into one or more of these categories.
Categorization (a cognitive operation in itself) can be done by the students, which keeps the process neat, since when a teacher does this for
them, problem solving by the student is interrupted. (How would you
elicit this from your students? What question would you ask? Which
words would you use to invoke the act of categorizing without doing it
for them?)

A "second inning" can start by focusing on each specific category:
"What are some more political reasons for man's revolt?" or "What
could be some more personal reasons?" It is very likely that more and
more reasons will be identified for each category. A new category may be
discovered in the process. At this point you might want to engage in the
act of "going beyond" or "stretching the limits." Suppose you ask the
following: "What would be the most unusual reason for man's revolt in
any of these categories?" or "What would be the most ludicrous reason?"
or "the funniest reason?" or "the most immoral reason?" or "the most
moral reason?", etc.

From here you can move to the aspect of *consequences* of a revolution, the consequences of each of the proposed solutions. Problems can
be designed to deal with revolutionary strategies, ways to prevent a revolution, ways to cope with it, advantages and disadvantages of change,
and many more facets.

Can you imagine the wealth of materials that will accumulate up to this point? Can you see that all these problems invite divergent thinking? Can you see that the various categories represent *subconcepts* within the *concept* of revolution, and that the content of each category is clusters of facts, different kinds of facts? You could now focus on a *particular* category (subconcept); you and your students might inquire into the meaning, reasons, nature, structure of political revolutions, or personal revolutions, or etc. The problems designed will focus on that category.

The next "inning" will include problems in the search for clusters, and *then* the finding of facts — historical, social, political, and other facts for each of the solutions previously proposed by the students. This can be done by reading (the students search for facts, the teacher supplies bibliographies. *Now,* not before, is the time to read.), by interviewing, by collecting revolution stories, etc.

At this stage (weeks may have passed for the development of the process) it may be feasible and desirable (if the students feel it so) to establish the *attitude* of *each* student toward a *specific* revolution. This will require the next step, that each student establish the *criteria* for his personal attitude, and fit each point of his criteria to the previously developed information and knowledge about the concept of revolution. Now the teacher may join the class in expressing a point of view, sets of attitudes — a value system. This final step can take the form of a debate, group discussion, lectures by individual students, mimeographed reports, slides, models, exhibits, or whatever.

Implications of Problem Solving

Risk Taking

Let us deviate slightly from the implication chart used in previous styles and single out the issue of *risk taking*. Problem Solving as a teaching style requires Problem Solving as a learning style. This transaction creates conditions of risk for both teacher and student. For the first time, decisions about subject matter are made by the learner, not preconceived by the teacher. (In Guided Discovery the learner makes decisions about subject matter in the impact-set; but the *consequences* of these decisions are predesigned by the teacher. In Problem Solving, the learner makes decisions not about *reproduction* of subject matter but about the *production* of alternative and other *new* subject matter.) This creation of subject matter has potential risks which require at least three levels of adjustments by teacher, student, or both.

The first adjustment is *philosophical*. Any rigid commitment to orthodox truth and right and wrong may be disturbed by different or new true or correct solutions. Teachers so committed find it difficult to accept alternative solutions—for example, the mathematics teacher who rejects a correct solution just because it is not his or may be an unfamiliar way of solving the problem.

Students accustomed to rigid rights and wrongs given to them by parents, teachers, religious leaders, etc., often find it difficult and risky to seek out new solutions; they feel safe within the realm of known materials. Confronted with the possibility of the unknown, anxiety and the fear of risk creep in; philosophically, they cannot go beyond what they know to be right.

The second level of adjustment is *cognitive.* In certain subjects students often come up with solutions beyond the teacher's cognitive experiences. This creates risk for the student, because teachers who cannot adjust to the realization of student's cognitive expansion invariably resort to retaliatory behavior.

The third level of adjustment, which probably encompasses the other two, is *emotional.* These cognitive and philosophical threats or challenges often make the teacher uncomfortable, distrustful, and, in the extreme, give a feeling of inadequacy. A teacher in this condition, threatened by potential risks, may resort to retaliatory behavior.

Perhaps the most important aspect of Problem Solving in relation to risk is the emergence of *individuality.* The weaning process that began with the shift from the Command to the Task Style, the beginning of deliberate individuali*zation* in instruction and learning, culminates in the beginning of individuali*ty,* the overt expression of the individual's unique ability to perceive, to think, to find out, to solve.

Implication for the Developmental Channels

The emergence of individuality moves the student on the developmental channels. A student who has learned to cope with the risks involved in the process of Problem Solving and the production of alternative solutions has advanced closer to the maximum in development on each of the channels *except* the social channel, because solving and thinking are private acts, though their expression is social. Significant emotional advances must take place in order to be able to be a problem solver. The student must *feel* that he *can* handle both the problem and the solutions produced for it. The affective and cognitive domains seem to be intricately interrelated during Problem Solving, due to the balance between emotional self-protection and cognitive arousal and production of alternatives.

To sum up this style let's review the schematic shift in decision mak-

Theoretical Limits Concept

Command Style	Task Style	Reciprocal Style	Individual Program	Guided Discovery	Problem Solving
Minimum ←					→ Maximum
Physical development					X
	?				
Social development	X				
Emotional development					X
Intellectual development					X

ing through the anatomy of the various styles. (Still evident is the tenacity of the teacher's decision-making role in the pre-impact set—the only decision set that has remained unchanged.)

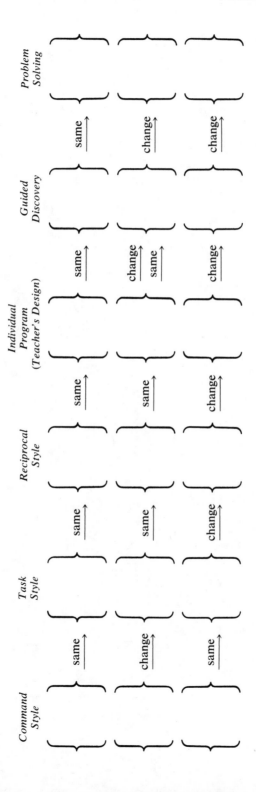

9

The Individual Program (Student's Design) or Toward Creativity

In Guided Discovery the student became involved in making decisions about subject matter, by employment of particular cognitive processes which terminated at every step in the desired, preplanned response.

In Problem Solving, while the teacher designed the problems (perhaps the last stronghold of control), the student was involved in a new emotional state which permitted freer cognitive flow. Moreover, beyond the mere individualization process (only in time, speed, rhythm, space, etc.) of previous styles, Problem Solving invokes *individuality* — perhaps the most significant difference between this style and its predecessors on the spectrum. *Problem Solving not only offers license to be different, it elicits, develops, and maintains the different and the unique.* Indeed, Guided Discovery and Problem Solving are two distinct processes within that of discovery. In one, the student discovers what others want him to discover, in the other he discovers what he can within the *area* that others have selected for him. But in the anatomy of these styles, although decisions about the *responses* are the student's, the *stimulus* (pre-impact subject-matter) decisions are the teacher's. The next step on the spectrum will create another condition for decision making by the student, the third style of discovery, and that is a shift in the pre-impact decisions concerning subject matter. The student will make *all* the decisions, in a condition of independence, will design the problems and ask the questions, all the questions.

The student's mind and feelings now know no boundaries, and work by emotional courage and cognitive freedom. A new level of reality is precipitated, stimulated by imagination, by hunches, by strange feelings, by obscure drives, by unusual thoughts.

Although the Individual Program (Student's Design) is the most open-ended, and by definition provides the student with the greatest level of freedom in decision making, some guide lines are offered for its operation in the classroom.

The major decision-making shift is in the pre-impact set; decisions about subject matter are now the student's. He must make decisions:

1. About his area of interest within the broad boundaries of the subject matter currently under study.
2. About *some* specific topics within that area of interest.
3. About the process for collecting, organizing, recording, and retrieving information.
4. About how to use and integrate self-generated ideas with the information gathered from other sources. This step is often quite crucial in the evolution of an independent project. The assessment of the relative value of the creative act is what interferes with the flow of ideas. During this phase of the student's decision making, the teacher must refrain from *any* evaluative statement. It is important to maintain the climate of free experimentation and exploration, by the teacher's acknowledgment rather than evaluation. At times it is best to keep away from the student altogether. Independent work, involvement in one's own cognitive production and creation requires a high level of privacy. If help is needed the student will seek it out. At this stage on the spectrum the student knows when the teacher is needed.
5. About the product, about the final form of the accumulated information and the creative substance. The final product might be a report, booklet, exhibit, movie, video-tape production, play, concert, transparencies, model, and many others. The focal point is a decision about the medium for communication with other people.

This kind of independent creative behavior also requires time—perhaps several weeks or months (indeed, on a higher level, years). This dimension calls for considerable adjustment in our view of the relationship between time and production, usually called efficiency. We are accustomed to see students engaged, sometimes busy, in familiar activities. Independent creative behavior treats time differently. There are periods of *seeming* non-production, usually the time needed for thinking, contemplation, or just floating along the cognitive streams which are invisible and often remote. At time the activities seem to be scattered, "unorganized." It is the very nature of the creative process to scatter, to jump, to take obscure roads. Time is required for the student to put order in the divergent creations of his mind, and that will be a kind of order (or organization) as perceived by the student. We often marvel at the ingenuity of students in organizing ideas on models they create, in experiments they design, in music they write.

Let us remember that the destiny of human knowledge, and perhaps human existence, has always been pushed to the brink of another level, another depth, another direction by people who dared, people who had the emotional strength and the cognitive freedom to question, to defy, to

Decision Shift to Student for Each Style

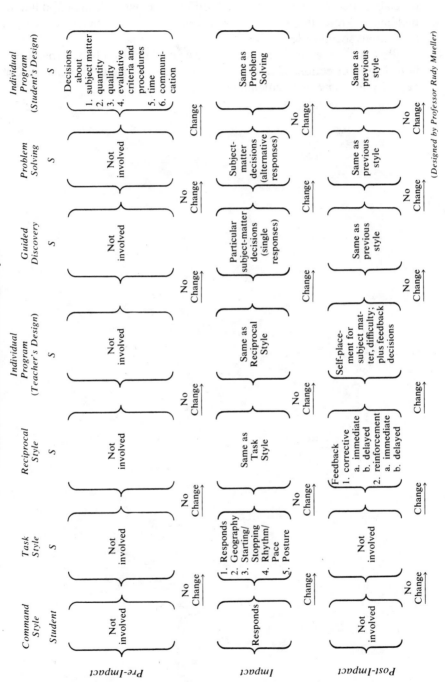

	Command Style	Task Style	Reciprocal Style	Individual Program (Teacher's Design)	Guided Discovery	Problem Solving	Individual Program (Student's Design)
	Student	S	S	S	S	S	S

Pre-Impact
- Command Style: Not involved / No Change
- Task Style: Not involved / No Change
- Reciprocal Style: Not involved / No Change
- Individual Program (Teacher's Design): Not involved / No Change
- Guided Discovery: Not involved / No Change
- Problem Solving: Not involved / No Change
- Individual Program (Student's Design): Decisions about 1. subject matter 2. quantity 3. quality 4. evaluative criteria and procedures 5. time 6. communication

Impact
- Command Style: Responds / Change
- Task Style: Responds 1. Geography 2. Starting/Stopping 3. Rhythm/Pace 4. Posture / No Change
- Reciprocal Style: Same as Task Style / No Change
- Individual Program (Teacher's Design): Same as Reciprocal Style / No Change
- Guided Discovery: Particular subject-matter decisions (single responses) / Change
- Problem Solving: Subject-matter decisions (alternative responses) / No Change
- Individual Program (Student's Design): Same as Problem Solving

Post-Impact
- Command Style: Not involved / Change
- Task Style: Not involved / No Change
- Reciprocal Style: Feedback 1. corrective a. immediate b. delayed 2. reinforcement a. immediate b. delayed / Change
- Individual Program (Teacher's Design): Self-placement for subject matter, difficulty; plus feedback decisions / No Change
- Guided Discovery: Same as previous style / No Change
- Problem Solving: Same as previous style / No Change
- Individual Program (Student's Design): Same as previous style

(Designed by Professor Rudy Mueller)

proclaim. People who composed different music, designed different buildings, wrote different books, invented new machines, conceived alternative social orders.

Perhaps we, as teachers, can make a small contribution in that direction, in the direction of freeing the capacities of man. Perhaps we can begin by teaching from command to discovery.

References

1. Allport, Gordon W. *Becoming*. New Haven: Yale University Press, 1955.
2. Allport, Gordon W. *Personality and Social Encounter*. Boston: Beacon, 1960.
3. Amidon, E. J., and J. B. Hough. *Interaction Analysis Research and Theory*. Palo Alto, Ca.: Addison-Wesley, 1971.
4. Anderson, R. C., and D. Ausubel. *Readings in the Psychology of Cognition*. New York: Holt, 1965.
5. Anderson, R. C. "Educational Psychology." *Annual Review of Psychology*. Vol. 18 (1967).
6. Berliner, D. C. *Microteaching and the Technical Skills Approach to Teacher Training*. Stanford Center for Research and Development in Teaching Technical Report #8. Palo Alto, Ca.: Stanford University.
7. Bower, G. H. "An association model for response and training variables in paired-associate learning." *Psychology Review*. 69 (1962), 34–53.
8. Broudy, H. S., O. B. Smith, and J. R. Burnett. "Education and the Uses of Knowledge," in Donald Vandenberg, ed. *Theory of Knowledge and Problem of Education*. Urbana, Ill.: Univ. of Illinois Press, 1969.
9. Bruner, J. S., J. J. Goodnow, and G. A. Austin. *A Study of Thinking*. New York: Wiley, 1960.
10. Bruner, J. S. *On Knowing: Essays for the Left Hand*. Cambridge, Mass.: Harvard University Press, 1962.
11. _____. *Toward a Theory of Instruction*. W. W. Norton and Co., N.Y., 1966.
12. Bruner, J. S. "The Act of Discovery." *The Harvard Educational Review*. XXXI (1961), 21–32.
13. Cook, J. O. "Superstition in the Skinnerian." *American Psychologist*. 18 (1963), 516–518.
14. Cronbach, L. J., and R. E. Snow. *Individual Differences in Learning Ability as a Function of Instructional Variables*. Report to the U.S. Office of Education (OEC 4-6-061269-1217). Stanford, Ca.: School of Education, Stanford University, 1969.
15. Ekstein, R., and L. M. Rocco. *From Learning for Love to Love of Learning*. New York: Brunner/Mazel, 1969.
16. Festinger, Leon. *The Theory of Cognitive Dissonance*. Evanston, Ill.: Row, Peterson, 1957.
17. Flanders, N. A. *Analyzing Classroom Behavior*. Palo Alto, Ca.: Addison-Wesley, 1965.
18. Gage, N. L. *Handbook of Research in Teaching*. Chicago: Rand McNally, 1963.
19. _____. "Toward a Cognitive Theory of Teaching." *Teachers College Record*. LXV (1964), 408–12.
20. Gagné, R. *The Conditions of Learning*. New York: Holt, 1965.
21. _____. "Varieties of Learning and the Concept of Discovery" in

Shulman and Keislar, eds. *Learning by Discovery*. Chicago: Rand McNally, 1966.

22. Glaser, Robert. "Variables in Discovery Learning," in Shulman and Keislar, eds. *Learning by Discovery*. Chicago: Rand McNally, 1966.

23. Goffman, Erving. *Stigma*. Englewood Cliffs, N.J.: Prentice-Hall, 1963

24. Guilford, J. P. *The Nature of Human Intelligence*. New York: McGraw-Hill, 1967.

25. Hamachek, D. E., ed. *The Self in Growth, Teaching and Learning*. Englewood Cliffs, N.J.: Prentice-Hall, 1965.

26. Harlow, H. F. "The Formation of Learning Sets." *Psychological Review*. LVI (1949), 51–65.

27. Holland, J. G. "Cook's Tour de Farce." *American Psychologist*. 19 (1964), 683–684.

28. Inhelder, B., and J. Piaget. *The Growth of Logical Thinking from Childhood to Adolescence*. New York: Basic Books, 1958.

29. Katona, George. *Organizing and Memorizing*. New York: Columbia University Press, 1949.

30. Leonard, George. *Education and Ecstasy*. New York: Delacorte, 1968.

31. Mager, R. F. *Preparing Instructional Objectives*. Belmont, Ca.: Fearon, 1962.

32. Maslow, A. H. "Some Educational Implications of the Humanistic Psychologies." *Harvard Education Review* (Fall 1968).

33. Mosston, Muska. *Inclusion and Exclusion in Education*. Somerville, N.J.: INEDCO Press, 1970.

34. Mosston, Muska, and Rudy Mueller. "Mission, Omission and Submission in Physical Education." NCPEAM Proceedings, Chicago (published by University of Minnesota), 1970.

35. Mosston, Muska. *Thinking and Moving*. Belmont, Ca.: Wadsworth (forthcoming).

36. Moustakas, C. E. "True Experience and the Self," in D. E. Hamachek, ed. *The Self in Growth, Teaching and Learning*. Englewood Cliffs, N.J.: Prentice-Hall, 1965.

37. Polya, G. *How to Solve It*. New York: Doubleday, 1957.

38. Raths, Louis, *et al. Teaching for Thinking: Theory and Application*. Columbus, Ohio: Merrill, 1967.

39. Schwebel, M. *Who Can be Educated?* New York: Grove, 1968.

40. Shulman, L. S., and E. R. Keislar. *Learning by Discovery*. Chicago: Rand McNally, 1966.

41. Skinner, B. F. *The Technology of Teaching*. New York: Appleton-Century-Crofts, 1968.

42. Suppes, P., and R. Ginsberg. "Application of a Stimulus Sampling Model to Children's Concept Formation with and without Overt Correction Response." *Journal of Experimental Psychology*. 63 (1962), 330–336.

43. Taba, Hilda. "Implementing Thinking as an Objective in Social Studies," in Jean Fair, Fannie R. Shaffel, eds. *Effective Thinking in the Social Studies*, 37th Yearbook, National Council for Social Studies.

44. Taylor, Calvin W. "Questioning and Creating: A Model for Curriculum Reform." *The Journal of Creative Behavior*. Vol. 1. No. 1 (January 1967).

45. Terrace, H. S. "Discrimination Learning With and Without Errors." *J. Exp. Anal. Behav.*, 1963a, 6, 1–27.
46. *TIP, Theory Into Practice.* Columbus, Ohio: Ohio State University. Vol. VII, No. 1 (February 1968). (An issue devoted to pressures on children.)
47. Torrance, P. E. *Encouraging Creativity in the Classroom.* Dubuque, Iowa: Wm. C. Brown, 1970.
48. Tumin, Melvin. "Popular Culture and the Open Society in *Mass Culture.*" Edited by Rosenberg, Bernard, and White, The Free Press, Glencoe, Ill., 1957.
49. Van Cleve, Morris. "Personal Choice," in D. Vandenberg, ed. *Teaching and Learning.* Urbana, Ill.: Univ. of Illinois Press, 1969.

Bibliography

Allen, Dwight W., and Kevin Ryan. *Microteaching*. Reading, Mass.: Addison-Wesley, 1969.

Allport, G. W. *The Nature of Prejudice*. New York: Anchor, 1954.

_____. *Pattern and Growth in Personality*. New York: Holt, 1961.

_____. *The Person in Psychology*. Boston: Beacon, 1968.

Almy, Millie. *Young Children's Thinking*. New York: Teachers College Press, Columbia University, 1966.

Anderson, H. *Creativity and Its Cultivation*. New York: Harper, 1959.

Ausubel, David P., and Floyd G. Robinson. *School Learning*. New York: Holt, 1969.

A.S.C.D. "A Climate for Individuality," Washington, D.C.: A.S.C.D.–N.E.A., 1955.

A.S.C.D. *Creating a Good Environment for Learning*. Washington, D.C.: National Education Association, 1954.

A.S.C.D. *Humanizing the Secondary School*. Washington, D.C.: National Education Association, 1969.

A.S.C.D. *Individualizing Instruction*. Washington, D.C.: A.S.C.D. 1964 Yearbook.

A.S.C.D. *Perceiving Behaving Becoming*. Washington, D.C.: A.S.C.D. 1962 Yearbook.

Ashton-Warner, Sylvia. *Teacher*. New York: Bantam, 1963.

Association for Childhood Education International. *Children Can Work Independently*. Washington, D.C.: The Association, 1952.

Baker, S. S. *Your Key to Creative Thinking*. New York: Harper, 1962.

Barkan, M., and R. L. Mooney, eds. *The Conference on Creativity: A Report to the Rockefeller Foundation*. Columbus, Ohio: Ohio State Press, 1964.

Bigge, Morris. *Learning Theories for Teachers*. New York: Harper, 1964.

Bloom, Benjamin S. *Stability and Change in Human Characteristics*. New York: Wiley, 1964.

_____. ed. *Taxonomy of Educational Objectives, The Classification of Educational Goals Handbook I: Cognitive Domain*. New York: McKay, 1956.

Bourne, L. E., Jr. *Human Conceptual Behavior*. Boston: Allyn and Bacon, 1966.

Brehn, J. W., and A. R. Cohen. *Exploration in Cognitive Dissonance*. New York: Wiley, 1962.

Bruner, J. S. *The Process of Education*. New York: Vintage, 1963.

_____. *Toward a Theory of Instruction*. Cambridge, Mass.: The Belknap Press of Harvard University Press, 1966.

_____, R. R. Olver and P. M. Greenfield. *Studies in Cognitive Growth*. New York: Wiley, 1966.

Bugental, J., ed. *Challenges of Humanistic Psychology*. New York: McGraw-Hill, 1967.

Burkhart, R. C. *Spontaneous and Deliberate Ways of Learning.* Scranton, Pa.: International Textbook, 1962.

Carin, A., and R. B. Sund. *Teaching Science through Discovery.* Columbus, Ohio: Merrill, 1964.

Cartwright, Dorwin, and Alvin Zander. *Group Dynamics.* New York: Harper, 1953.

Cofer, C. N., and M. H. Appley. *Motivation: Theory and Research.* New York: Wiley, 1964.

Cohea, Dorothy H., and Virginia Stern. *Observing and Recording the Behavior of Young Children.* New York: Teachers College Press, Columbia University, 1967.

Collins, Barry E., and Harold Guetzkow. *A Social Psychology of Group Processes for Decision Making.* New York: Wiley, 1964.

Cremin, Lawrence A. *The Genius of American Education.* New York: Vintage, 1965.

Cunningham, Ruth. *Understanding Group Behavior of Boys and Girls.* New York: Bureau of Publications, Teachers College, Columbia University, 1951.

Commission on Teacher Education. *Helping Teachers Understand Children.* Washington, D.C.: American Council on Education, 1945.

Dennison, George. *The Lives of Children.* New York: Random, 1969.

Deutsch, Morton. "An Experimental Study of the Effects of Cooperation Competition upon Group Process," *Journal of Human Relations,* Vol. II, No. 1, 1949.

_____. "A Theory of Cooperation and Competition," *Journal of Human Relations,* Vol. II, No. 2, 1949.

Dewey, John. *Democracy and Education.* New York: Macmillan, 1916.

_____. *Experience and Education.* New York: Collier, 1938.

_____. *How We Think.* Boston: Heath, 1933.

_____. *Theory of Valuation.* Chicago: University of Chicago Press, 1939.

Dixon, T. R., and D. L. Horton, eds. *Verbal Behavior and General Behavior Theory.* Englewood Cliffs, N.J.: Prentice-Hall, 1968.

Eble, Kenneth E. *A Perfect Education.* New York: Macmillan, 1966.

Elkind, David. "Piaget and Montessori," *Education Digest,* 33 (March 1968), 43–46.

Ellis, H. *The Transfer of Learning.* New York: Macmillan, 1965.

Engelmann, Siegfried and Therese. *Give Your Child A Superior Mind.* New York: Simon and Schuster, 1966.

Erikson, Erik H. *Childhood and Society.* New York: Norton, 1950.

Escalona, Sibylte. *The Roots of Individuality.* Chicago: Aldine, 1968.

Eyl, J. B. "General Conditions of Child Thought," *Catholic Editors Review,* 66 (1968), 184–195.

Festinger, L., and Daniel Katz. *Research Methods in the Behavioral Sciences.* New York: Holt, 1953.

Fisher, Dorothy Canfield. *The Montessori Manual.* Cambridge, Mass.: Robert Bentley, 1964.

Flanders, N. A. *Inaction Analysis in the Classroom: A Manual for Observers.* Lithographed, University of Michigan, 1960.

Flavell, John H. *The Developmental Psychology of Jean Piaget.* Princeton: Van Nostrand, 1963.

Flemming, R. S., and R. C. Doll. *Children under Pressure.* Columbus, Ohio: Merrill, 1966.

Fowler, Harry. *Curiosity and Exploratory Behavior.* New York: Macmillan, 1965.

_____, G. W. Ford, and L. Pugno, eds. *The Structure of Knowledge and the Curriculum.* Chicago: Rand McNally & Co., 1964.

Frandsen, Arden N. *Educational Psychology,* 2nd Ed. New York: McGraw-Hill, 1967.

Furth, Hans G. "Concerning Piaget's Views on Thinking and Symbol Formation," *Child Development,* 39 (1968), 997–1001.

_____. *Piaget and Knowledge.* Englewood Cliffs, N.J.: Prentice-Hall, 1969.

_____. "Piaget's Theory of Knowledge: The Nature of Representation and Interiorization," *Psychological Review,* 75 (1968), 143–154.

Gardner, John W. *Excellence—Can We Be Equal and Excellent Too?* New York: Harper, 1961.

Getzels, Jacob W., and Philip W. Jackson. *Creativity and Intelligence: Exploration with Gifted Children.* New York: Wiley, 1962.

Gibson, Janice. *Educational Psychology: A Programmed Text.* New York: Appleton-Century-Crofts, 1968.

Ginott, Haim. *Between Parent and Child.* New York: Macmillan, 1965.

Goffman, Erving. *Presentation of Self in Everyday Life.* New York: Doubleday, 1959.

Good, Carter V. *Introduction to Educational Research.* New York: Appleton-Century-Crofts, 1959.

Goodlad, John, and Robert Anderson. *The Nongraded Elementary School.* New York: Harcourt, 1959.

Goodman, Mary Ellen. "Through the Eyes of Young Children," *Parents,* 43 (July 1968), 35–37.

Gordon, Ira J. *Human Development: From Birth through Adolescence.* New York: Harper, 1962.

_____. *Human Development: Readings in Research.* Chicago: Scott, Foresman, 1965.

_____. *Studying the Child in School.* New York: Wiley, 1966.

Gordon, Sol, ed. *Pressures That Disorganize in Secondary Schools,* 31st Yearbook, 1966, N.J. Secondary School Teachers Association.

Guilford, J. P. "Factors That Aid and Hinder Creativity," *Teachers College Record,* LXII (February 1962), 380–392.

_____. *Fundamental Statistics in Psychology and Education.* New York: McGraw-Hill, 1965.

_____. *Personality.* New York: McGraw-Hill, 1959.

_____. *Psychometric Methods,* 2nd Ed. New York: McGraw-Hill, 1954.

_____. "Three Faces of Intellect," *The American Psychologist,* Vol. 14 (August 1959).

Halsey, Elizabeth. *Inquiry and Invention in Physical Education.* Philadelphia: Lea & Fibiger, 1964.

Hartmann, Heinz. *Essays on Ego Psychology*. New York: International Universities Press, 1964.

Harper, F. J., C. C. Anderson, C. M. Christensen, S. W. Hunka. *The Cognitive Processes Readings*. Englewood Cliffs, N.J.: Prentice-Hall, 1964.

Hebb, Donald O. *Organization of Behavior*. New York: Wiley, 1949.

_____. *A Textbook of Psychology*. Philadelphia: W. B. Saunders Company, 1958.

Hilgard, Ernest F., and Gordon H. Bower. *Theories of Learning*. New York: Appleton-Century-Crofts, 1966.

Holt, John. *How Children Fail*. New York: Dell, 1970.

_____. *How Children Learn*. New York: Dell, 1970.

Hooper, Frank H. *Logical Thinking in Children*. New York: Holt, 1968.

Hunt, McV. J. *Intelligence and Experience*. New York: Ronald, 1961.

Hyman, Ray. *The Nature of Psychological Inquiry*. Englewood Cliffs, N.J.: Prentice-Hall, 1964.

Irwin, Leslie W. *The Curriculum in Health and Physical Education*. St. Louis, Mo.: The C. V. Mosby Co., 1951.

Jones, Richard. *Fantasy and Feeling in Education*. New York: New York University Press, 1968.

Kagan, Jerome. "The Child," *Saturday Review* (December 7, 1968), pp. 80–82, 87–88.

Kessler, Jane W. "Taking the Mis out of Misbehavior," *P.T.A. Magazine*, 63 (October 1968), 10–12, 34.

Kimble, Daniel P., ed. *The Anatomy of Memory*. Palo Alto, Calif.: Science and Behavior Books, 1965.

Klausmeier, H. J., and W. Goodwin. *Learning and Human Abilities*. New York: Harper, 1966.

_____, and Chester W. Harris, eds. *Analyses of Concept Learning*. New York: Academic Press, 1966.

Kleinmuntz, Benjamin. *Problem Solving*. New York: Wiley, 1966.

Koffka, Kurt. *The Growth of the Mind*. New York: Harcourt, 1924.

Krathwehl, David R., Benjamin S. Bloom, and Bertram B. Masia. *Taxonomy of Educational Objectives, the Classification of Educational Goals, Handbook II Affective Domain*. New York: McKay, 1964.

Landreth, Catherine. *Early Childhood: Behavior and Learning*. 2nd Ed. Knopf, 1967.

Levin, D., ed. *Nebraska Symposium on Motivation*. Lincoln, Nebraska: University of Nebraska Press, 1964.

Logan, Frank A., and Allen R. Wagner. *Reward and Punishment*. Boston: Allyn and Bacon, 1965.

Long, Nicholas. "Helping Children Cope with Feelings," *Childhood Education*, 45 (1969), 367–372.

Lorenz, Konrad. *On Aggression*. New York: Bantam, 1966.

_____. *Evolution and Modification of Behavior*. Chicago: Phoenix, 1967.

Lowenfeld, Viktor, and W. Lambert Brittain. *Creative and Mental Growth*. 4th Ed. New York: Macmillan, 1964.

Lysaught, Jerome, and Clarence M. Williams. *A Guide to Programmed Instruction*. New York: Wiley, 1963.

Manis, M. *Cognitive Process*. Monterey, Ca.: Brooks/Cole, 1966.

Marksberry, Mary Lee. *Foundation of Creativity.* New York: Harper, 1963.

Maslow, Abraham. "Criteria for Judging Needs To Be Instinctoid," in M. R. Jones, ed. *Human Motivation: A Symposium.* Lincoln, Nebraska: University of Nebraska Press, 1965.

_____, ed. *New Knowledge in Human Values.* New York: Harper, 1959.

_____. "Self-actualization and Beyond," in J. Bugental, ed. *Challenges of Humanistic Psychology.* New York: McGraw-Hill, 1967.

_____. *Toward a Psychology of Being* (Revised Edition). Princeton, N.J.: Van Nostrand, 1968.

McCandless, Boyd. *Children and Adolescents: Behavior and Development.* New York: Holt, 1967.

McDonald, Frederick J. *Educational Psychology.* 2nd Ed. Belmont, Ca.: Wadsworth, 1965.

McGaugh, James L. "Some Changing Concepts about Learning and Memory," N.E.A., 57 (April 1968), 8–9.

McLuhan, Marshall. *Understanding Media.* New York: Signet, 1964.

Mehler, Jacques, and Thomas G. Beaver. "Cognitive Capacity of Very Young Children," *Science,* 8 (October 6, 1967), 141–142.

Miel, Alice, ed. *Creativity in Teaching.* Belmont, Ca.: Wadsworth, 1961.

Miller, G., E. Galanter, and K. Pribram. *Plans and the Structure of Behavior.* New York: Holt, 1960.

Mitzel, H. E., and Rabinowitz. *Reliability of Teachers' Verbal Behavior. A Study of Withall's Technique for Assessing Social-Emotional Climate in Classroom.* Publication 15. College of the City of New York, Division of Teacher Education, Office of Research and Evaluation, 1953.

Mosston, Muska. *Developmental Movement.* Columbus, Ohio: Merrill, 1965.

_____. *Problem Solving—A Problem for Educators.* Somerville, N.J.: INEDCO Press, 1970.

Moustakas, C. *The Authentic Teacher.* Cambridge, Mass.: Howard A. Doyle, 1966.

Mood, A. M. *Introduction to the Theory of Statistics.* New York: McGraw-Hill, 1950.

Mueller, Rudy. *A Learning Climate for Children Who Cannot.* Somerville, N.J.: INEDCO Press, 1970.

Murphy, Gardner. *Human Potentialities.* New York: Basic, 1958.

Muse, M. B. *Guiding Learning Experiences.* New York: Macmillan, 1950.

Myers, R. E., and E. P. Torrance. "Can Teachers Encourage Creative Thinking?" *Educational Leadership,* XIX (1961), 156–159.

National Society for the Study of Education. "Programmed Instruction," *NSSE Yearbook,* LXVI, Pt. II. Chicago: The University of Chicago Press, 1967.

Neill, A. S. *Summerhill.* New York: Hart, 1960.

New Jersey Secondary School Teachers Association. *Pressures That Disorganize in Secondary School.* N.J. Secondary School Teachers Association Yearbook, 1966.

Newton, Suzanne. "How to Encourage Your Child's Natural Creativity," *Parent,* 43 (July 1968) 42–43.

Patrick, Catherine. *What Is Creative Thinking?* New York: Philosophical Library, 1955.

Peter, Laurence. *Prescriptive Teaching.* New York: McGraw-Hill, 1965.

Phillips, J. L., Jr. *The Origins of Intellect: Piaget's Theory.* San Francisco: W. H. Freeman, 1969.

Piaget, Jean. *The Construction of Reality in the Child.* New York: Basic Books, 1960.

—————. *Judgment and Reasoning in the Child.* New York: Humanities Press, 1952.

—————. *Language and Thought of the Child.* New York: Humanities Press, 1955.

—————. "Mapping the Growing Mind," *Time* (December 12, 1969), p. 61.

—————. *The Moral Judgment of the Child.* New York: The Free Press, 1965.

—————. *The Origins of Intelligence in Children.* New York: Norton, 1963.

—————. *Psychology of Intelligence.* New Jersey: Littlefield, Adams and Co., 1963.

—————. *Six Psychological Studies.* New York: Random, 1967.

Piaget, Jean, and Barbel Inhelder. *The Growth of Logical Thinking.* New York: Basic Books, 1958.

—————. *The Psychology of the Child.* New York: Basic Books, 1969.

Polos, Nicholas. *The Dynamics of Team Teaching.* Dubuque, Iowa: W. C. Brown Co., 1965.

Prescott, Daniel A. *The Child in the Educative Process.* New York: McGraw-Hill, 1957.

Rapaport, David. *Organization and Pathology of Thought.* New York: Columbia University Press, 1959.

Redl, Fritz. *When We Deal with Children.* New York: Free Press, 1966.

Richter, Derek, ed. *Aspects of Learning and Memory.* New York: Basic Books, 1966.

Robins, Lee N. *Deviant Child Grown Up.* Baltimore, Md.: Williams and Wilkins, 1966.

Rogers, Carl. *On Becoming a Person.* Boston: Houghton Mifflin, 1961.

Rosenberg, Marshall. *Diagnostic Teaching.* Seattle, Wash.: Special Child Pub., 1968.

Russell, D. *Children's Thinking.* Chicago: Ginn Book Co., 1956.

Sanford, Nevitt. "Creativity and Learning," *Daedalus* (Summer 1965).

—————. "Education For Individual Development." Washington, D.C.: Annual Meeting of the American Orthopsychiatric Association, 1967.

Sarbin, Theodore R., and Vernon L. Allen. "Increasing Participation in a Natural Group Setting: A Preliminary Report," *Psychology Record,* 18 (1968), 1–7.

Schon, Donald A. "The Fear of Innovation," *International Science and Technology,* No. 59 (November 1966).

Sears, Pauline S. and Vivian S. Sherman. *In Pursuit of Self-Esteem.* Belmont, Ca.: Wadsworth, 1965.

Severin, F., ed. *Humanistic Viewpoints in Psychology.* New York: McGraw-Hill, 1965.

—————, and J. F. T. Bugental, eds. *Challenges of Humanistic Psychology.* New York: McGraw-Hill, 1967.

Shibutani, Tamotsu. "A Cybernetic Approach to Motivation," in Walter Buckley, ed. *Modern Systems Research For the Behavioral Scientist.* Chicago: Aldine, 1968.

Shulman, Lee S. and Evan R. Keisler, eds. *Learning by Discovery.* Chicago: Rand McNally, 1966.

Sigel, I. E., and Hooper, F. H. *Logical Thinking in Children.* New York: Holt, 1968.

Silberman, Charles E. *Crisis in the Classroom.* New York: Random, 1970.

Skinner, B. F. *Science and Human Behavior.* New York: Macmillan, 1953.

_____. *Verbal Behavior.* New York: Appleton-Century-Crofts, 1957.

_____. *Walden Two.* New York: Macmillan, 1960.

Smith, Karl U., and Margaret Foltz Smith. *Cybernetic Principles of Learning and Educational Design.* New York: Holt, 1966.

Smith, Othanel B. "A Conceptual Analysis of Instructional Behavior," *Journal of Teacher Education,* XIV (1963), 294–98.

Spence, K. W. *Behavior Theory and Learning.* Englewood Cliffs, N.J.: Prentice-Hall, 1960.

Spitz, Rene. *No and Yes: On the Genesis of Human Communication.* New York: International University Press, 1957.

Staats, Arthur W., and C. K. Staats. *Complex Human Behavior.* New York: Holt, 1963.

_____. *Human Learning.* New York: Holt, 1964.

_____. *Learning, Language and Cognition.* New York: Holt, 1970.

Standing, E. M. *The Montessori Method.* California: Academy Library Guild, 1962.

Stein, Morris I. *Identity and Anxiety.* New York: Free Press, 1960.

_____, and Shirley Heinze. *Creativity and the Individual.* New York: Free Press, 1960.

Stott, Leland H. *Child Development.* New York: Holt, 1967.

Taba, Hilda. *Curriculum Development Theory and Practice.* New York: Harcourt, 1962.

_____. *Teachers' Handbook for Elementary Social Studies.* Palo Alto, Ca.: Addison-Wesley, 1967.

_____. *Teaching Strategies for the Culturally Disadvantaged.* Chicago: Rand McNally, 1966.

Theory into Practice (TIP). College of Education, Ohio State University, VII, 1 (February 1968). (An issue devoted to pressures on children.)

Torrance, Paul E. *Education and the Creative Potential.* Minneapolis: University of Minnesota Press, 1963.

_____. *Guiding Creative Talent.* Englewood Cliffs, N.J.: Prentice-Hall, 1962.

_____. *Gifted Children in the Classroom.* New York: Macmillan, 1965.

_____. *Rewarding Creative Behavior.* Englewood Cliffs, N.J.: Prentice-Hall, Inc., 1965.

_____. "The Measurement of Creative Behavior in Children," *Productive Thinking in Education.* Ed. by Mary Jane Aschner and Charles E. Bish. NEA and Carnegie Corp. of New York, 1965.

_____. "What Research Says to the Teacher," *Creativity,* No. 28. Washington, D.C.. National Education Association, 1963.

Ulrich, R. Stachnik, and J. Mabry, eds. *Control of Human Behavior*. Chicago: Scott, Foresman, 1966.

Valenti, Carlo. "The Child," *Saturday Review* (Dec. 7, 1968), pp. 75–78.

Wertheimer, M. *Productive Thinking*. New York: Harper, 1954.

Wilhelms, Fred. *Evaluation as Feedback and Guide*. Washington, D.C.: ASCD, 1967.

Withall, J., J. M. Newell, and W. W. Lewis. *Use of Communication Model to Study Classroom Interaction*. Paper. American Educational Research Association, 1961.

Yinger, Milton J. *Toward a Field Theory of Behavior*. New York: McGraw-Hill, 1965.

Zirbes, Laura. *Spurs to Creative Thinking*. New York: Putnam's, 1959.

Index